THE GREAT RIGHTS

THE GREAT RIGHTS

Edited by
EDMOND CAHN

THE MACMILLAN COMPANY, NEW YORK
COLLIER–MACMILLAN LIMITED, LONDON

© New York University 1963

Second Printing, 1964

Printed in the United States of America

The Macmillan Company, New York
Collier-Macmillan Canada, Ltd., Toronto, Ontario

Library of Congress catalog card number: 63–14939

New York University School of Law,

sponsor of this volume, dedicates it to

THE LIVING SPIRIT OF JAMES MADISON

NEW YORK UNIVERSITY SCHOOL OF LAW
expresses its gratitude to

LOUIS SCHWEITZER

for the love of liberty, equality, and justice that prompted him to
endow the James Madison Lectures and foster the making of this
volume.

CONTENTS

THE GREAT RIGHTS

1

A NEW KIND OF SOCIETY

Edmond Cahn

I. THIS is a book about our original purpose as a nation and the way it stands today. At the start of our history, there were good patriots to whom the purpose was uncongenial. They saw no need for the new country to adopt new political aspirations. As far as they could see, the conflict that broke out in 1775 was no more than a War of American Independence, the stakes in the war were only the traditional rights of Englishmen, and the important passages in the Declaration which some of them signed in 1776 were those that listed their grievances against George III and the British Parliament. All the aims of men like these were good and fair, but far too narrow, too small. The world of the Founding Fathers felt ripe for something bolder than one more England in approximate replica on the western shores of the Atlantic.

Something daring and novel was in the wind which caught the finest minds of the time and inflamed them. To men like James Madison, the war against Britain was only the military aspect of an all-pervasive American Revolution[1] and the question to be decided was not whether Americans should regain the rights that Englishmen had considered customary but whether for the first time in human history any men anywhere could enjoy the full political dignity to which all men were born. Though English notions of liberty were obviously useful, they were inadequate. What America promised must be nothing less than a new kind of society—fresh, equal, just, open, free, and forever respectful of conscience.

3

The big question, as we know, was how to implement this vision and find constitutional machinery that would give it force. How does one go about protecting the basic rights that men ought to have in a free society? The answer was certainly not apparent in 1787. All that the Founding Fathers felt sure of was the need for something in writing. They never doubted that whenever a new nation emerged from the Egypt of repression or colonialism it should next find its own version of Mount Sinai and formally inscribe the tablets of its fundamental law. The English had obtained a Bill of Rights in 1689, Virginia had adopted a Declaration of Rights in 1776, and other states had followed the example. The very first step must consist in composing and adopting a text.

Of course, everyone including Jefferson (who eloquently demanded a national Bill of Rights) and Madison (who drafted it and steered it through the phases to final adoption) understood that it would not always prevail over the passion of the people, the arrogance of officials, or the insensibility of both. They knew that the best of texts could present only "parchment barriers"[2] against official aggression. What they observed in England and America was mainly discouraging. Almost without exception, whenever emotions, interests and impulses had mounted high, all the solemn exhortations adopted in sober times had counted for nothing. Magna Carta was a parasol but no umbrella, good on sunny days when few needed it, but useless in a storm.

Here came the first momentous breakthrough: the discovery that mere declarations, exhortations and wishful normatives would not suffice and that the situation called for flat commands. The English Bill of Rights was replete with "oughts" and "ought nots" addressed to the government, moral admonitions doomed to the usual fate of moral admonitions when they clashed with immediate interest. So too George Mason's Virginia Declaration of 1776, lofty in terms but feeble in effect because, as John Marshall described it, "merely recommendatory."[3]

4

This is why it is a revelation to watch the following sequence:

English Bill of Rights of 1689: "Excessive bail *ought not* to be required, nor excessive fines imposed; nor cruel and unusual punishments inflicted."

Virginia Declaration of Rights of 1776: "Excessive bail *ought not* to be required, nor excessive fines imposed, nor cruel and unusual punishments inflicted."

Amendment Proposed by Virginia Convention of 1788 that Ratified the Federal Constitution: "Excessive bail *ought not* to be required, nor excessive fines imposed, nor cruel and unusual punishments inflicted."

Amendment Proposed by Madison in Congress on June 8, 1789, Adopted as Eighth Amendment: "Excessive bail *shall not* be required, nor excessive fines imposed, nor cruel and unusual punishments inflicted."

The breakthrough came because Madison believed profoundly that in America the people were sovereign and the officials their mere trustees, agents and servants. He put it neatly. "In Europe," he wrote, "charters of liberty have been granted by power." And in America? "Charters of power granted by liberty."[4] In Magna Carta where King John, though acting under coercion of powerful nobles, nevertheless spoke as monarch, "We will not" was deemed fitting (in Latin, of course, for the benefit of the common man). In the English Bill of Rights where William and Mary, though accepting the conditions that Parliament had exacted, still spoke as sovereign, "ought not" was deemed bold enough for the protection of the rights of subjects. But when the American people in 1789 prescribed the acts that their new Federal Government must either not do or do only in a particular manner, they were entitled to say "shall not," the language of command. Thus, the old flaccid promises and pious exhortations were at last toughened into imperative law.

II.

This was only a first stage, though a momentous one, and two more remained before Madison's work would be done. Converting the exhortations of old English charters into peremptory commands of law was quite an accomplishment. Yet standing alone it could never equip the new kind of society because there was nothing in the charters about the rights that Americans prized highest. Nothing, even by way of exhortation, about the rights that would differentiate the new, open, democratic society from the stratified systems of the Old World: freedom of speech, freedom of the press. Nor was there any categorical guarantee of the free exercise of religion.[5]

Perhaps it was this last lack—the lack of religious freedom in the old country—that demonstrated most clearly, at least in Madison's eyes, the inadequacy of the English experience as a model for America. Like George Mason, whom he had assisted in drafting the Virginia Declaration of Rights of 1776, he did not hesitate to employ whatever was helpful in the English charters, for example, as we have just seen, the clause against "cruel and unusual punishments." But he had learned while working with Mason that the very highest of English ideals did not approach what he and Jefferson, among others, demanded on behalf of the religious conscience in America.

We can dispense with details. To describe the condition of English law, say from 1776 to 1789, governing the rights of religious minorities would be unnecessary and unkind. Suffice it to say that almost all the historic—yet not quite complete—steps that England has taken to grant civil and political equality to her Roman Catholic and Jewish subjects lay then in the future. Given the existence of the established national Church, the highest plane of religious freedom which even a John Locke could project for minorities was mere "toleration." Toleration was the distant goal, the English libertarian's summum bonum toward which he strived.

6

Apparently it seemed liberal enough to George Mason in 1776 when he prepared his initial draft of the Virginia Declaration of Rights. But not to young James Madison, who would have none of it. "Toleration," he submitted, was not the word for consciences; free men were "entitled" to their religions, and "equally" at that. Nobly acquiescing, Mason deleted all phrases of "toleration," substituted Madison's "all men are equally entitled to the free exercise of religion, according to the dictates of conscience," and submitted the Declaration to an approving legislature.

Thus it was that as early as 1776 Madison had devised new American materials to meet the needs of the new society. The commands and guarantees of the First Amendment that would enable Americans to speak freely, publish freely, and worship freely were too ambitious to be copied or derived; they had to be indigenous.

III.

When Madison had executed the initial step (converting exhortations into legal commands) and the second one (devising legal commands that would conduce to an open society), the constitutional mechanism was still incomplete. We know, of course, what remained to be established: that is, the judicial review of constitutionality. If the great guarantees were to become something more than alluring promises, it was evident that courts must enforce them by nullifying government action that violated them. Clearly, others too—the President, the Congress, civil officials, army officers, and the general citizenry—must also cooperate in observing, obeying, and enforcing them; ultimately the vitality of the guarantees might depend on the spirit of the whole nation. But, first and foremost, it was the judges who would play a decisive role which Madison put explicitly before the Congress:

7

If they [the rights] are incorporated into the constitution, independent tribunals of justice will consider themselves in a peculiar manner the guardians of those rights; they will be an impenetrable bulwark against every assumption of power in the legislative or executive; they will be naturally led to resist every encroachment upon rights expressly stipulated for in the constitution by the declaration of rights.[6]

Since this is what the Founding Fathers trusted and expected when they adopted the Bill of Rights, we may well ask: How much time and attention did the United States Supreme Court actually devote, during ensuing generations, to performing its "peculiar" guardianship of civil liberties? What proportion of the Court's business has had to do with freedom, equality, and the safeguards imposed on criminal justice? It is interesting to see what even a summary answer will show.

Until 1868, the Court's civil-liberty task was quite light because the Bill of Rights originally restricted only the *Federal Government*, which had few operations and functions in those days. During this initial period, the Court had time enough to embark on a different and very elaborate judicial enterprise, that is, it attempted, case by case, to construct a national system of common law to govern commercial transactions.[7]

In 1868 with the adoption of the Fourteenth Amendment, the Supreme Court received the additional function of protecting personal liberties against the *States*. From that time, a considerable number of civil-liberties and civil-rights cases knocked at the judges' door. The proportion that obtained admission was not impressive. Through the years the Court did make certain sturdy libertarian decisions but, at least after 1925 when an Act of Congress gave it wide discretion to choose the cases it would hear, it could have won much greater gains for human freedom if it had been less busy reviewing the wisdom and desirability of social and economic reforms enacted by the State and Federal Governments. Meanwhile, despite protests from Holmes and

8

Brandeis, the justices went on with their arduous, time-consuming attempt to build a national common law.

Two immense changes—one in 1937, the other in 1938—marked the beginning of the modern period. In 1937, responding to President Franklin D. Roosevelt's criticisms and his so-called "Court-packing Plan," the Supreme Court ceased acting like a third house of the legislature, resumed its former, very limited role in passing on acts of social and economic legislation, and permanently disclaimed any right to assess their desirability or undesirability. Since then, the justices have felt free not only to dismiss many elaborate constitutional challenges to regulatory legislation but also to curtail review of the relative few they do consider.

In 1938, the Court lopped another considerable element from its former jurisdiction. Holding that all its efforts—complex, tedious and protracted over a period of ninety years—to establish a national common law in commercial matters had been improper and unconstitutional, it jettisoned the entire enterprise.[8]

We need not wonder, then, that since 1938 the crowded calendar of the Supreme Court has accorded more room to cases involving civil rights and liberties. While commercial litigations still receive a fair share of the justices' attention, they are no longer displacing the concern with life and human freedom. By what it did in 1937 and 1938, the Court readied itself, as it were, to devote an ampler allotment of time, thought, study, and solicitude to the elementary rights of men. Since no previous allotment during any era of the Court's history came near to being adequate, one could reasonably say that the present generation of Americans is the very first to whom Madison's vision is within reach.

Shifts in the Court calendar would, of course, have little libertarian value if there were not so many concomitant signs of increased moral sensibility among the justices. Year by year, save only its mottled performance in the field of national security, the Court seems to bring deeper understanding, wider sympathy, and more intelligent analysis to the moral aspects of legal problems.

9

Increasingly, as befits the highest tribunal of a representative democracy, it examines the issues before it in the perspective of their manifold impacts on concrete persons and social aggregations, i.e., the consumer perspective. Often the Court demonstrates that one or another provision of the Bill of Rights is not only binding law, it is also good and true and morally right.

Take, for example, the clause with which we have become familiar: the one prohibiting "cruel and unusual punishments," which we traced back to 1689. Years ago, certain justices used to contend that the clause, having originated in 17th century England, forbade only those punishments which Englishmen of the seventeenth century considered "cruel" and that any subsequent advance in social practices and moral sensibilities was immaterial.[9] This would be one way, certainly not Madison's way, to construe the clause. The Court has proved that there is a much better way, which it applied in two of its recent decisions.

In the first of them, a twenty-year old soldier, serving during World War II in French Morocco, escaped from an army stockade where he had been confined and returned voluntarily the next day, explaining that he was cold and hungry. After suffering the full burden of a court-martial sentence which included three years at hard labor, forfeiture of pay, and a dishonorable discharge, he returned to civilian life and asked for a passport to travel. It was denied him because, according to a federal statute, his desertion had stripped him of American citizenship and left him stateless. He took his case to the Supreme Court, which held that to denationalize him and leave him without a country or a legal status anywhere would be cruel and unusual punishment.[10]

In the other case, the State of California—not content with enacting the usual sanctions against anyone who manufactures, uses, sells, etc. unauthorized narcotic drugs—went farther and made it a crime simply to be addicted to drugs. The statute criminalized the mere *status* or condition of addiction which, as the State itself recognized, was essentially a mental and physical illness. The Supreme Court struck down the California "addiction" law for inflicting cruel and unusual punishment.[11]

Decisions like these are beacons of the new society.

IV.

In order to enhance the appreciation of civil liberty and strengthen the sense of national purpose, New York University School of Law in 1960 established the annual James Madison Lectures. The main chapters of this book are based on the first four Lectures, delivered respectively by Justice Hugo L. Black, Justice William J. Brennan, Jr., Chief Justice Earl Warren, and Justice William O. Douglas. Lecturers in the series are selected from the federal judiciary.

The plan of the James Madison Lecture series contemplates a cycle of approximately twenty years. As the reader will see, the first four Lectures together present the *general philosophy* of constitutional liberty. For them, invitations were extended to jurists who were deemed most thoroughly imbued with Madisonian ideals and principles. The next sixteen Lectures will be devoted to *specific* guarantees in the Constitution and Amendments and *specific* enforcement problems (e.g., the treason clause, trial by jury, the equal protection of the laws, the standing to sue). Since a thorough re-examination of fundamental principles will be appropriate every twenty years, a new cycle will begin then and follow the same pattern.

Freedom is not free. Shaping and preserving a new kind of society necessarily involves personal commitment, costly risk, and constant effort; the cultivation of civil liberty can be no more passive than the cultivation of a farm. A man can inherit the land on which he lives, he can even inherit the first crop of produce after he takes over from those who came before him. But then if he stops, everything stops, and begins to crumble. Nothing grows, nothing ripe and rewarding comes to him, unless he plows, plants and tends the soil and unless he keeps it fertile year after year with the chemistry of effort and forethought. Nor will he retain the harvest it yields unless, while he gathers and reaps, he exerts himself to repel trespassers and aggressors with indomitable will. It requires resolution, faith and courage to maintain what Madison called "the great rights of mankind."[12]

2

THE MADISON HERITAGE

Irving Brant

IN A journal of the proceedings of Congress kept briefly by James Madison, the following entry closes the record for that American year of destiny, 1787: "May 2 . . . I left New York for the Convention to be held in Philadelphia."

The Congress in New York was the body officially known as "The United States in Congress Assembled," which with steadily diminishing strength, or steadily increasing feebleness, sought to rule the eleven-year-old United States of America. The Convention was the one that drafted the Constitution under which "We the people of the United States" have ruled and been governed from 1789 down to the present moment—the oldest written and still living charter of government in the world.

In New York, the thirty-six-year-old Virginia delegate to Congress and the Convention had been working assiduously on the preliminaries to the Philadelphia meeting. If someone with a penchant for preserving objects of historical interest had taken possession of a certain table or desk in the boarding house of Mrs. Dorothy Elsworth, at No. 19 Maiden Lane, it could be pointed to today as one on which the "Father of the Constitution" performed half a dozen notable services in the course of earning that well-merited though often misunderstood title:

1. Here, in the spring of 1787, Madison wrote his analytical "Vices of the Political System of the United States." This was devoted to exposure of the manifold evils in state governments and the decline of national authority after the early period of wartime unity and power, a decline which he attributed to "the defect of legal & coercive sanctions" in the Articles of Confederation.[1]

2. Here too, Madison put on paper the fruits of a year-long study "Of Ancient & Modern Confederacies"—a warning to the United States to avoid the errors that had prostrated the three confederacies of ancient Greece (the Lycian, the Amphyctionic and the Achaean) as well as the Helvetic, Belgic and Germanic confederacies of modern Europe.[2]

3. Here also, in April of 1787, he outlined the principles and

structure of a new national government in nearly identical letters[3] to Governor Edmund Randolph of Virginia, titular head of the state's seven-man delegation to the Philadelphia gathering, and to George Washington, who was in everybody's mind for president of the Convention. Those letters contained the substance of the Virginia Plan, drawn by Madison, approved by the Virginia delegation, presented to the Convention by Governor Randolph, and adopted by it as the foundation on which to build a government. Its fifteen resolutions embodied the basic principles and structure of the final charter.[4]

4. Returning to New York in the following September, Madison took the lead in securing a unanimous decision by Congress to submit the proposed constitution to the states for ratification. Unanimity was obtained, after a stormy debate, through Madison's counsel of moderation: to submit the document without a recommendation for or against it.

5. After that, in spite of urgent calls to return to Virginia and combat the powerful antifederalist leadership of Patrick Henry, Madison remained in New York through February 1788, officially as a delegate to Congress, but chiefly to take part with Alexander Hamilton and John Jay in the writing of the famous series of newspaper articles, expounding and advocating the Constitution, which took their place in history as the *Federalist Papers*.

6. A year later, in New York once more as a Virginia representative in the First Congress of the United States, Madison again took up his pen in Mrs. Elsworth's boarding house. There he drafted the first ten amendments to the Constitution and prepared the written outline, fortunately preserved to this day, of the crucially important speech delivered by him in submitting the amendments to Congress on June 8, 1789.[5]

The Madison Heritage is an emanation from his entire adult life, from early manhood to the last months of his eighty-five years, but there is scarcely a part of it that did not find expression in those three formative years of American government, from 1787 through 1789, which he spent in New York City. Philadelphia's Independence Square was rightly made a national historical monument, as the birthplace of the Declaration of Independence and the Constitution of 1787. But it was in New York City, below Washington Square, that the principles and basic structure of our present government were formulated. It was there that they were explained and expounded to the nation. It was there that guarantees of the rights and liberties of the people, called for by the ratifying conventions, were formally incorporated in the new national charter. In all of the preliminary and subsequent actions in New York, as well as in the central task of constitution-building in Philadelphia, the mind and spirit of James Madison furnished not only a creative but in many respects a dominant influence.

Human history is full of paradoxes. Among them few are more remarkable than the fact that the American Revolution was begun and carried through by men who were essentially conservative in their political thinking and economic leanings, yet who challenged aristocratic institutions and pinned their faith on representative self-government based on the great body of the people. It is a serious error, but a common one, to draw too sharp a distinction between the statesmen ordinarily tagged as conservatives, such as Washington, John Adams, Hamilton, Ellsworth, Jay and Marshall, and those classified as liberals or radicals—Jefferson, Madison, Franklin, Samuel Adams, George Mason, Patrick Henry. There were wide differences in the degrees to which they supported democratic principles under the republican form of government; differences also in their relative emphasis on human rights and property rights. But these—important though they are—were gradations in a general devotion to the principles set forth in the opening paragraph of the Declaration of Independence, to whose maintenance all of them pledged their lives, their fortunes and their sacred honor.

From this it follows (though the fact is evident anyway upon analysis) that there is no such conflict in spirit as some people think they see between the Declaration of Independence and the Constitution. Equally erroneous is the widespread belief that the first ten amendments to the Constitution, guaranteeing civil rights and liberties, are in sharp contrast with a main document from which guarantees of that type were callously omitted. The complete American Bill of Rights contains approximately half a hundred guarantees of rights and liberties, of which no less than sixteen can be counted in the body of the Constitution, twenty-five in the first ten amendments, and eight in amendments subsequently adopted.

James Madison approached his service to the country through the twin gates of the American Revolution and zeal for freedom of religion. His family shared in the general American paradox found in those days of ferment. James Madison, Sr., largest landholder of Orange County, Virginia, owner of a hundred slaves, justice of the peace, vestryman of the established Anglican church, was as solid a specimen of the landed gentry as anyone could ask for. He also was strongly opposed to establishment of an American Episcopate, which would have tied the church in Virginia to an English hierarchy, and he became head organizer of Orange County's armed resistance to England.

There was no family opposition, therefore, when in 1768 James Madison, Jr., chose the (New Light Presbyterian) College of New Jersey (now Princeton University) in preference to a Virginia institution whose president was a reputed candidate for the Episcopacy. Had the Church of England been established in the Northern colonies as it was in Virginia, young Madison wrote to a friend, "it is clear to me that slavery and subjection might and would have been gradually insinuated among us."[6]

Madison's preparation for public service actually began in childhood. By the age of fifteen, after five years in the Virginia school conducted by Donald Robertson, he was thoroughly grounded in the Latin classics, was familiar with Socrates, Plato, Montesquieu, Locke, Euclid, Copernicus, Descartes, Berkeley, and had a reading knowledge of French and Spanish. Of Robertson he said long afterward: "All that I have been in life I owe largely to that man."[7] At Princeton, Madison had the good fortune to come in contact with a scholar and teacher—President John Witherspoon, lately arrived from Scotland—whose forte, aside from theology, was the Law of Nations and of Nature. Through him, the young Virginian became acquainted with the works of Grotius, Pufendorf, Burlamaqui, and Vattel. Montesquieu's *Spirit of Laws* was a classroom textbook, but Voltaire had to be read surreptitiously. David Hume, whose writings stirred Witherspoon's almost unlimited capacity for anger, made a profound and lasting impression on Madison, and through him on American institutions of government.

The two years Madison needed to do four years' work at Princeton did not so much complete his education as give him the knowledge of how to acquire one and intensify the will to do so. Returning to the family estate, Montpelier, he spent the next three years in deeper study of public law, combined with the spirited support of the American patriots who were gradually moving toward revolutionary resistance to British rule. Near at hand he saw other conditions, inherent, as he believed, in any state afflicted with an established church. To his friend William Bradford in Philadelphia he wrote:

> Poverty and luxury prevail among all sorts; pride, ignorance, and knavery among the priesthood, and vice and wickedness among the laity. This is bad enough, but it is not the worst I have to tell you. That diabolical, hell-conceived principle of persecution rages among some; and to their eternal infamy, the clergy can furnish their quota of imps for such business.[8]

The Quaker Commonwealth came much closer than the Old Dominion to Madison's ideas on freedom of religion. As he expressed it to Bradford: "That liberal, catholic, and equitable way of thinking, as to the rights of conscience, which is one of the characteristics of a free people, and so strongly marks the people of your province, is but little known among the zealous adherents to our hierarchy." His friend was fortunate to dwell in a land where the public had "long felt the good effects of their religious as well as civil liberty." Foreigners had been encouraged to settle there, promoting industry and virtue by mutual emulation. In Pennsylvania's free air, "commerce and the arts have flourished, and I cannot help attributing those continual exertions of genius which appear among you to the inspiration of liberty, and that love of fame and knowledge which always accompany it." In contrast, "Religious bondage shackles and debilitates the mind, and unfits it for every public enterprise, every expanded prospect."[9]

Here Madison combined intense devotion to religious freedom, which he saw under immediate attack all about him, with broad support of civil liberties as a whole. He could see cultural as well as material benefits in the arrival of German, Irish and Scotch-Irish immigrants, then being welcomed in Pennsylvania and barely tolerated in Virginia. His approach to religious, social, political and economic matters was marked by a sweeping catholicity where human beings were concerned, and by a conspicuous lack of geographic provincialism. He was an American rather than a Virginia patriot, but he did not exalt native Americans above persons of foreign birth who came to the country seeking liberty and opportunity.

In 1776, at the age of twenty-five, Madison was sent as an Orange County delegate to Virginia's first revolutionary convention, thus beginning an almost uninterrupted forty years of public life. Frail of body and modest to the point of shyness, he might with his background of youthful thinking have been expected to give silent endorsement to George Mason's article on religious toleration in the convention's Declaration of Rights. Instead, he pointed out in committee a defect which at that time was practically universal in such guarantees. In Mason's draft the state, possessing power to do the opposite, graciously allowed dissent from the established religion. Madison recast this into a declaration that "all men are equally entitled to the free exercise of religion, according to the dictates of conscience." The convention, with Mason's hearty approval, accepted the change, but the committee rejected a further clause proposed by Madison that would have disestablished the church and prohibited state aid to religious teachers. The time had not come for so drastic a departure from custom.

In 1780, after intervening years as a state legislator and as a member of the Governor's Council directing war operations, Madison entered the Continental Congress. Here his continental outlook gave a national cast to his revolutionary zeal. Observing that the once all-powerful Congress was sinking into impotence because of the astronomical inflation of continental currency, he tried to induce that body to assert and use implied powers in the Articles of Confederation to compel the states to obey congressional requisitions of money. These efforts failing, he took the lead in attempts to grant effective powers to Congress by amendment of the Articles. Unanimous ratification was needed, and one state thwarted the effort.

Like nearly all revolutionary leaders from George Washington down, Madison habitually referred to the United States as a nation from the time of the adoption of the Declaration of Independence. Few, however, matched the vigor of his language in denying the individual sovereignty of the states. He was shocked to the core when he read that Henry Laurens, sent as American minister to Holland and captured by the British en route, had presented a humble petition to Parliament to be released from the Tower of London. If Laurens actually signed that petition, Madison said on the floor of Congress, he had "prostrated the dignity of his Country, wounded its honour, and as far as in him lay denied its sovereignty and independence." Such a petition, Madison told his colleagues, would be unworthy of a private citizen. Far worse to have it come from a minister "commissioned to represent the Sovereignty of these United States." The appeal "is stated not as coming from a citizen of the United States but a native of South Carolina. What is this but indirectly relinquishing the Claim of Independence which we have so solemnly declared and pledged ourselves to maintain at the risque of our lives and fortunes?"[10] Laurens, former President of Congress, was successfully defended by South Carolina delegates, not on the basis of state sovereignty, but as the excusable victim of fourteen months of imprisonment, solitude, illness and despair.

It was fortunate for the country that the Confederation's "three-year rule" forced Madison to leave Congress at the end of 1783. Elected at once to the Virginia legislature, he worked in that arena to strengthen the federal government, initiated a state program of waterway development, tried unsuccessfully to uphold the peace treaty of 1783 against debt-dodging violators, and won the hardest fight of his life in defense of religious freedom. Under Madison's leadership, the House of Delegates rejected Patrick Henry's heavily-favored bill for state support of all teachers of the Christian religion—a palpable scheme to bribe dissenting sects to support a broadened substitute for the tithe system struck down by Jefferson some years earlier. Henry's bill, postponed for a year by strategic maneuvering, died without even a vote on it—buried under the thousands of signatures to Madison's "Memorial and Remonstrance Against Religious Assessments."

In this memorial, Madison asserted that the right of conscience proclaimed in the Virginia Declaration of Rights—his own clause—"is in its nature an unalienable right"—unalienable because the opinions of men cannot follow the dictates of other men; because "what is here a right towards men, is a duty towards the Creator"; because every man who enters civil society owes a prior allegiance to the Universal Sovereign. "We maintain therefore that in matters of Religion, no man's right is abridged by the institution of Civil Society, and that Religion is wholly exempt from its cognizance."[11]

Under Madison's reasoning, freedom of conscience was infringed by any form of state support of religion. Henry's bill, entitled "A Bill establishing a provision for Teachers of the Christian Religion" was therefore a violation of the state's Declaration of Rights. But it would be invalid even without such a constitutional provision, because religion is totally outside the purview of civil government.

While Madison was waging and winning this fight, the Confederation was swirling toward dissolution—a Congress without taxing power pleading in vain for funds from the states, and the states employing their exclusive power over commerce as an instrument of desperate commercial warfare against their neighbors. To avert the threatened national collapse, Madison induced the Virginia legislature to issue a call for the Annapolis Convention of 1786. In that poorly attended and abortive meeting, designed to lead to congressional power over commerce and impost duties, Madison joined Alexander Hamilton in promoting a call for a general convention to revise the whole structure of federal government, to be held in Philadelphia in May, 1787. The response was quickened by the fear-inspiring musket-and-pitchfork rebellion of debt-ridden Massachusetts farmers under Daniel Shays. Madison needed no such prod to action, but others did.

In his "Vices of the Political System of the United States," Madison laid stress on the derelictions of the states—their refusal to comply with constitutional requisitions of money, their encroachment on federal authority, their violations of treaties, the multiplicity, mutability and injustice of state laws. So far had these evils progressed, he wrote, that they brought into question "the fundamental principle of republican Government, that the majority who rule in such governments are the safest Guardians both of public Good and private rights."[12]

Expressing for the first time a thought he rephrased again and again, Madison observed that all civilized societies are divided into different interests and factions, as they happen to be creditors or debtors, rich or poor, farmers or merchants or manufacturers, members of different religious sects, followers of different political leaders, owners of different kinds of property, etc. Whenever a common interest or passion united a majority, there was need of some form of restraint to prevent unjust violations of the rights and interests of the minority. Where was that restraint to be found without the sacrifice of republican government?

Madison rejected ethics and religion as restraining influences on legislatures. On the contrary, such considerations were even more commonly disregarded by assemblies than by individuals. *Security of private rights could be found only in a larger sphere of society*, one so large that in it conflicting interests, pursuits and passions would check each other. This conclusion, suggested by the writings of Hume, was directly contrary to the preachment of Montesquieu that virtue in a republic is inversely proportionate to its size. Amplifying his thought, Madison concluded that a federal government thus automatically restrained, also checked and balanced within itself and vested with authority to control the excesses of the states, would bring stability and justice to the entire republic. This was the central idea that Madison took with him when he left New York for Philadelphia on May 2, 1787. It underlay the provisions of his Virginia Plan, and was extensively set forth by him in debate.

To put this overall system into effect, it was imperative to frame the new federal government in accord with the opening affirmative declaration of the Virginia Plan: "Resolved . . . that a *national* Government ought to be established consisting of a *supreme* Legislative, Executive & Judiciary."[13] (Italics in original.) The word "national" was explained to mean a government bearing directly on the people, rather than (as in the Confederation) chiefly on the states as members of a federal union. But the word "supreme" had all the legal force and meaning it possesses in Article VI of the Constitution. The creation of a federal government, including a federal judiciary, *supreme over the states and state governments within the full range of constitutional provisions,* was in Madison's mind before he left New York. Approval of it was the first constructive action of the Philadelphia convention.

The Virginia Plan declared that Congress ought to enjoy all the legislative rights included in the Articles of Confederation (notably those involving war and peace, common defense, treaties, diplomacy, maritime law, coinage, postal service, Indian affairs, interstate territorial disputes) and "moreover to legislate in all cases to which the separate state are incompetent, or in which the harmony of the United States may be interrupted by the exercise of individual Legislation."[14] At the moment, Madison told the convention delegates, he was uncertain whether that clause should go into the Constitution or serve as a guide in the framing of enumerated powers. He had a strong bias in favor of an enumeration, but grave and increasing doubt of its feasibility. The resolution was adopted without deciding on that point.

Later, Madison joined in the decision to enumerate the federal powers and offered additions to those that came from the Committee on Detail, but his original resolution still serves as an index to the intended scope of national authority. Any constitutional construction that upholds the power of Congress in a field where individual state action is incompetent to its ends, or where it may produce disharmony in the United States, is in accord with the underlying purposes of the framers as Madison defined them and the convention declared them. That does not write the declaration of intent into the Constitution, but it creates a broad presumption against the existence of any vacuum between federal and state power, and an equally broad presumption of constitutionality wherever state incompetence or state-engendered disharmony can be brought within the implications of an enumerated power. That, almost by definition, embraces the wide area in which federal power has been supported by constitutional interpretation during the past 170 years, to the dismay of strict constructionists, including some instances in which Madison opposed the logical consequences of his own thinking.

Great as were Madison's services in the substantive framing of the Constitution (the work, he called it, "of many heads and many hands"), his most important single contribution was in the realm of persuasion. It was due largely to him that the men of substantial wealth who made up the Federal Convention were induced to entrust their property interests to a government broadly based on representative democracy. Madison's widely-shared distrust of the states found expression in many curbs on them—most notably in the subordination of state courts and legislatures to the federal judiciary and in the clause forbidding impairment of contracts—but when a motion was made to extend this last restriction to Congress it was not even seconded. Half a dozen delegates, including Benjamin Franklin, spoke out more strongly than Madison in support of a broad suffrage, but it was his argument about the safety and stability of a balanced federal republic of large extent that dissipated the almost universal fear of democratic violence—a fear rendered acute by Shays' Rebellion—and won the support of men who needed to be convinced.

The right of suffrage, Madison said in debate,[15] was a fundamental article of republican government. Gradual restriction of it, when left to legislative discretion, was the method by which popular governments were turned into aristocracies. Viewing the subject on merit alone, he regarded freeholders as "the safest depositories of Republican liberty," because a day would come when a great majority of the people, rendered landless and without other property, would either unite for the destruction of property rights or subvert public liberty by becoming the tools of opulence and ambition. In spite of holding this opinion, Madison voted against a freeholder restriction in the Constitution because it would narrow the suffrage in several states where voting rights were broader than in his own. Long afterward, in a commentary on this very speech, he repudiated the restrictive argument entirely, saying he had been too much influenced by Virginia's example. Such a limitation, he wrote, "violates the vital principle of free Government that those who are to be bound by laws, ought to have a voice in making them. And the violation would be more strikingly unjust as the lawmakers become the minority."[16]

Had Madison been that sort of person, he could have escaped the need of explaining that 1787 deviation from democratic principles by a very simple device—merely expunging it from his own record of his remarks. That he did not do so illuminates one of the noblest features of the Madison Heritage.

Besides taking a larger share than any other person in the fifteen weeks' proceedings of the Constitutional Convention, Madison doubled his work by keeping a daily record of its debates. Held secret (by the expressed will of the Convention) for half a century, it furnishes today the only full contemporary record of what went on behind those closed doors and is a leading guide to the intentions of the framers. Madison had this record in his closet during many years in which, owing to disclosure by others of his 1787 hostility to state sovereignty, he was subjected to violent criticism in a Southern society stirred to frenzy by the struggle over slavery. He revised his manuscript booklet with pasted inserts made from the official Journal, published in 1819, and with interlinings derived from the fragmentary notes of Robert Yates, published in 1821. In correspondence he parried the quotations by Yates that revealed his antistate attitude, without overt denial of them, by treating the New Yorker's frequent opinionated exaggerations as evidence of total unreliability. But he let his own record of his nationalistic position stand, for posthumous publication, to damn him in a society that employed State Rights to keep a subject race in bondage, and to exalt him, ultimately, among those who seek human equality and economic democracy along the road of federal power.[17]

Madison looms so large in the record from which constitutional opinions are formed that his probity is a matter of capital importance. A well known professor of law in a western university, whose unique interpretation of the Constitution requires the discrediting of the Notes of Debates, published the charge a few years ago (without supporting evidence) that Madison in his old age interpolated fourteen fictional speeches in the debate on the clause dealing with state export or import duties (article I, section 10, clause 2). The alleged purpose of this supposed action was to aid the spread of slavery in the territories (to which Madison was unsympathetic) by creating an inference that the Slave Trade prohibition (article I, section 9, clause 1) applied (as it assuredly did) only to importation of slaves *from abroad*. That was indeed a feat for Madison to perform: to imitate, page after page, the departed handwriting of his youth. And how superfluous, when all he needed to do was insert two words, "from abroad," in the brief debate on the Slave Trade clause itself.

The allegation also has been made (though not yet published) by a scholar who examined the manuscript of Madison's Notes of Debates, that the entries for the last week of August 1787 were written and inserted many years afterward. The evidence is that the handwriting is not that of his youth, but displays the irregularities typical of advancing age. It does have that appearance, but the explanation lies elsewhere. On August 23 Madison was stricken with an illness that almost cost him his life. In spite of it he lost not a day from his self-assumed task, and his handwriting straightened out when he recovered. No better evidence is needed that the manuscript in the vaults of the Library of Congress is the original, written out while the Convention was in progress.

In the writing of *The Federalist* (from which John Jay soon dropped out because of illness) the two principal authors made no set division of subjects in the eighty papers they poured out, fifty-one by Hamilton, twenty-nine by Madison. But it is easily observable that Madison devoted himself much more than Hamilton to the principles of republican government, to the fundamental rights of citizens, and to the arrangements designed to assure stability and justice to all classes without infringing the rights of individuals. His classic discussion of the causes of faction, in the Tenth Federalist, gives first but not sole place to economic factors in the formation of political parties. It presents the remedy which he himself implanted in the American system —offsetting one interest by another through representative government by the people, federally organized in many subordinate and one supreme and far-flung jurisdiction. A religious sect, he said, might degenerate into a political faction, but diversity of sects furnished security against danger. "A rage for [unbacked] paper money, for an abolition of debts, for an equal division of property, or for any other improper or wicked project, will be less apt to pervade the whole body of the Union, than a particular member of it. . . ."[18] Closely related to this in Madison's thinking was his exposition in the Fifty-first Federalist of the constitutional separation of powers and the system of checks and balances. Throughout his life he regarded this as a final expression of his views on the proper organization of republican government for the joint ends of justice, safety and effectiveness.

Again and again, in *The Federalist*, Madison lays stress on "the great body of the people" as the necessary source of all authority in a truly republican commonwealth. "It is *essential* to such a government," he wrote in No. 39, "that it be derived from the great body of the society, not from an inconsiderable proportion, or a favored class of it"; otherwise "a handful of tyrannical nobles" might delegate their powers to pretended representatives and exercise their oppressions under the honorable title of a republic.[19] Again, in No. 57, Madison dealt with the trumped-up fear that members of the House of Representatives would be chosen from the class of citizens having least sympathy with the mass of the people.

"Who," he exclaimed, "are to be the electors of the federal representatives? Not the rich, more than the poor; not the learned, more than the ignorant; not the haughty heirs of distinguished names, more than the humble sons of obscurity and unpropitious fortune. The electors are to be the great body of the people of the United States."[20]

In the Federal Convention, Madison had emphasized the *magnitude* of the powers to be transferred to the national government, embracing virtually all the attributes of sovereignty. In *The Federalist*, writing to allay the fear that the states were being swallowed up, he emphasized the *fewness* of the powers transferred and said nothing about their magnitude. But in this appeal to the people he made no understatement of the significance of the clause empowering Congress to make all laws necessary and proper to carry the delegated powers into effect. Without that authority, he asserted, the whole Constitution would be a dead letter. And the power would exist even if not set forth, because "no axiom is more clearly established in law, or in reason, than that wherever the end is required, the means are authorized; wherever a general power to do a thing is given, every particular power necessary for doing it, is included."[21] Chief Justice Marshall merely paraphrased that in his more famous definition of the clause.

Marshall once said that of all the public men he had ever known, Patrick Henry had the greatest power to persuade, Madison the greatest power to convince. On another occasion Marshall remarked that if eloquence included the art of "persuasion by convincing, Mr. Madison was the most eloquent man I ever heard."[22]

Marshall had taken an important part in the debates of the Virginia convention of 1788, wherein Madison and Patrick Henry led the rival forces supporting and opposing ratification of the new Constitution. Henry found fresh terrors in every constitutional clause. Madison, again weakened by fever, could scarcely be heard by the delegates who crowded close around him. Yet he laid the mighty orator low by calm, steady, logical analysis, reducing the fiery dragons of Henry's imagination to vapory wisps. Considering Virginia's pre-eminent position among the states, first in prestige, first in population, first in physical power, first in size, bisecting the entire country from the Atlantic coast to the Mississippi River, it may well be doubted whether ratification by nine states without Virginia would have brought the new government actually into effect. Like his contribution to *The Federalist*, Madison's service in the ratifying convention was not only a decisive factor in the preservation of the Union by reform of its government; it was a proof of the immeasurable gain to the nation when intellect rates higher than glamor in the public reaction to the political competition between them in a period of crisis.

The one rational fear voiced by Virginia opponents of the Constitution—voiced most effectively by George Mason—arose from the absence of a specific Bill of Rights. Scattered through the original Constitution are guarantees of that nature. The right of habeas corpus is protected; jury trials are required in criminal cases; treason trials limited; bills of attainder and ex post facto laws prohibited; religious tests for office forbidden; titles of nobility banned. But George Mason's motion for a Bill of Rights, designed especially to cover religious and other freedoms, was rejected as unnecessary. The Constitution, it was said, delegated no power to Congress to interfere with such rights.

Belief soon spread—propagated especially by those who wanted the Constitution defeated for other reasons—that the framers rejected Mason's motion because of indifference or hostility to the rights themselves. But George Washington wrote to Lafayette, months before Virginia acted on the Constitution, that "there was not a member of the [Philadelphia] convention, I believe, who had the least objection to what is contended for by advocates for a Bill of Rights."[23] Madison remarked at a later day that the delegates were less considerate of Mason's desires than they would have been had he raised the issue earlier in the Philadelphia proceedings. Haste and fatigue in the closing days of the Convention, he said, were factors in the adverse decision.

The opinions of Washington and Madison find support in the contrast between the cursory dismissal of Mason's proposal, made only three days before the Constitution was formally adopted and ordered engrossed, and the affirmative action some weeks earlier on a motion that Congress be forbidden to pass bills of attainder or ex post facto laws. Two future Justices of the Supreme Court (Ellsworth and Wilson) argued that the prohibition of ex post facto laws was unnecessary—"there was no lawyer, no civilian who would not say that *ex post facto* laws were void of themselves." That part of the clause was adopted by a divided vote, on the argument that unhappy experience with legislatures "overruled all calculations." This written prohibition was something "the judges can take hold of." The remainder of the clause was unanimously approved, with Gouverneur Morris (by no means renowned for devotion to civil liberties) declaring that a constitutional prohibition was unnecessary as to ex post facto laws "but essential as to bills of attainder." That clause came from men who knew and feared such instruments of tyranny.[24]

In the Virginia ratifying convention, delegates who wanted the Constitution rejected demanded amendment of it *before ratification*—a sure method of putting it to death. To combat this move, Madison and his allies minimized the need for specific guarantees, contending that Congress lacked power to interfere with the rights of individuals and that faulty or inadequate definition of those rights might create danger where none existed. But, Madison said, he would be willing to recommend amendments along that line, to be submitted by Congress *after ratification*, if the Virginia convention thought them necessary. It did, and the Constitution was ratified on that understanding.

In the following winter, as a candidate for Congress, Madison had to deal with a whispered antifederalist canard, aimed at the

Baptists he had so long been defending, that he had abandoned the cause of religious freedom. Ratification of the Constitution without *prior* attempts at alteration, he wrote to his chief supporter in that sect, had made the move for *subsequent* amendments both safe and proper:

> Under this change of circumstances, it is my sincere opinion that the Constitution ought to be revised, and that the first Congress meeting under it ought to prepare and recommend to the States for ratification, the most satisfactory provisions for all essential rights, particularly the rights of Conscience in the fullest latitude, the freedom of the press, trials by jury, security against general warrants etc. . . . and to put the judiciary department into such a form as will render vexatious appeals impossible.[25]

Soon after the First Congress convened in New York City, Madison sounded out Federalist members (a term applied at that time to friends of the Constitution) and found many of them inclined to delay. Let more important measures come first, they said. Early in June he learned that the Antifederalists were planning to seize the initiative, intending to seek damaging substantive changes as well as libertarian guarantees. Giving advance notice, he took the floor on June 8, said he felt "bound in honor and in duty" to place amendments before the House, and asked permission to do so on that day, lest unfounded suspicions inflame the public mind against the decisions of Congress. His appeal won, and he proceeded at once to present, explain and advocate his sheaf of amendments.[26]

From this source came the first ten amendments of the Constitution, including those guaranteeing freedom of religion, speech, press, petition and assembly; restricting unreasonable search, seizure and warrants of arrest; providing that no person be deprived of life, liberty or property without due process of law, and giving ten other specific protections to accused persons. These include the right to a speedy and public trial by jury, the right to counsel, to be confronted with accusing witnesses, to be protected against self-incrimination and against being placed twice in jeopardy for the same offense.

In subsequent debate on the tenth amendment, Madison successfully resisted an attempt to insert one word, to make it say that the powers not *expressly* delegated to the United States are reserved to the states or the people. No government, he contended, could be limited to express powers: "there must necessarily be admitted powers by implication."

One proposal, called by Madison "the most valuable amendment in the whole list," provided that "no State shall violate the equal rights of conscience, or the freedom of the press, or the trial by jury in criminal cases." The Constitution, he said, wisely and properly forbade the states, as well as Congress, to pass bills of attainder or ex post facto laws. The same double interdiction ought to extend to these other great and important rights. Even though they were already protected in most state constitutions, nothing could give a more sincere proof of attachment to them than to have state and federal governments join in doubling the security. Where freedom of religion and freedom of the press are concerned, "it is proper that every Government should be disarmed of powers which trench upon those particular rights."[27]

This amendment, approved by the House, was dropped by the Senate. Eighty years later, the main protections thus sought came into existence through the fourteenth amendment, whose due process clause is construed to bar the states from violating the freedoms set forth in the first amendment. Thus the fourteenth amendment is in the line of the Madison Heritage, but even more important is the language employed in presenting the original proposal to Congress.

The guarantees of the first amendment, and indeed of the entire Bill of Rights, are subject today to a process of judicial erosion. There is a dangerous and growing tendency in the Supreme Court, both in upholding these rights and in denying them, to look upon them as mere precepts, to be observed or disregarded according to the exigencies of the moment. The words of the Constitution, "Congress shall make no law . . . abridging the freedom of speech," are balanced against the evils (which the founders of our nation had learned were lesser ones) inherent in the right to speak freely. The doctrine we are threatened with is that if, in some particular circumstance, the value of suppressing a guaranteed freedom seems of greater moment than the right to exercise that freedom, the plain words of the Constitution may be disregarded.

That construction reveals an almost incredible misconception of the purpose and value of the first amendment. Overt incitement to disorder or outrages against decency can be taken care of without perverting the Constitution by subtle misconstruction. The men who placed the guarantee of free speech in the Constitution were not authorizing Congress to choose between its protection and its suppression by a comparison of values. Their concern was with the fundamental basis of all self-governing societies—the right of the people to think, speak, write, publish and assemble without the menacing shadow of government over them. It is that whole broad inherent right—the right to freedom of thought, expression and association in a democratic republic—that was weighed and chosen in 1789, against the possible value of some particular suppression. When that choice is left in balance, it is no longer a choice but a decision against free government.

Madison knew the danger of legislative violence in periods of emotional upset. It was for that reason that he sought double security for freedom of religion and press in the Constitution. That was why he wanted *"every Government disarmed of powers which trench upon those particular rights."*[28] (Emphasis added.) There is no disarmament of government in the doctrine of balance between the right of the individual to speak and of Congress to forbid him to do so.

35

When Madison wrote, "Congress shall make no law" infringing these rights, he did not expect the Supreme Court to decide, on balance, whether Congress could or could not make a law infringing them. It was true, he observed in presenting his proposals, that state legislative bodies had violated many of the most valuable articles in bills of rights. But that furnished no basis for judging the effectiveness of the proposed amendments:

> If they are incorporated into the Constitution, independent tribunals of justice will consider themselves in a peculiar manner the guardians of those rights; they will be an impenetrable bulwark against every assumption of power in the Legislative or Executive; they will be naturally led to resist every encroachment upon rights expressly stipulated for in the Constitution by the declaration of rights.[29]

This statement by Madison, along with all the rest of his speech, is so devastating to the "balance theory" that efforts have been and are being made to discredit its authenticity. The *Annals of Congress*, it is said, is not an official document, but a compilation of stenographic reports (by a shorthand reporter admitted to the floor for that purpose) published in the press and containing numerous errors. That is true, although the chief complaint was that partially caught sentences were meaningless. In general, that which was clearly reported was truly reported. In the case of this all-important speech, Madison spoke from notes, and the notes in his handwriting are in the Library of Congress. They parallel the speech from end to end, scantily, but leaving no doubt of the fundamental faithfulness of the report.

Five years passed before Madison had occasion to discuss in Congress the application of constitutional guarantees of liberty. In 1794, during the political turmoil created by Pennsylvania's Whisky Rebellion, partisan charges were made that the Democratic Societies were concerned in it. Without naming them (that would have been quite too shocking) it was proposed to amend a resolution condemning the rebellion by inserting the following:

As part of this subject, we cannot withhold our reprobation of the self-created societies, which have risen up in some parts of the Union, misrepresenting the conduct of the Government, and disturbing the operation of the laws, and which, by deceiving and inflaming the ignorant and the weak, may naturally be supposed to have stimulated and urged the insurrection.[30]

Opinions, Madison told the House, are not objects of legislation. Criticize people for abusing their reserved rights and how far will it go? "It may extend to the liberty of speech, and of the press." He then showed how far it had already gone:

It is in vain to say that this indiscriminate censure is no punishment. If it falls on classes, or individuals, it will be a severe punishment. He wished it to be considered how extremely guarded the Constitution was in respect to cases not within its limits. . . . Is not this proposition, if voted, a vote of attainder?

Madison then laid down this general rule: "If we avert to the nature of Republican Government, we shall find that the censorial power is in the people over the Government, and not in the Government over the people."[31]

The resolution was defeated. Under the conditions prevailing in 1794, the condemnation by Congress of unnamed but identifiable societies might indeed have inflicted punishment. But how does that compare with the blanket accusations hurled by congressional committees today against named groups, or the pillorying of hundreds of individuals whose mere citation to appear before congressional committees is enough to blacken their reputations and menace or destroy their means of livelihood? By Madison's standard, as well as by that of the Supreme Court in *Cummings v. Missouri*,[32] bills of attainder are being enacted today against thousands of victims, by a government that has forgotten the principles of liberty on which it is built.

Madison's faith in "independent tribunals of justice" was sadly jolted when the Alien and Sedition Acts of 1798 received the approval of individual Supreme Court justices riding circuit. His

37

Virginia Resolutions of that year, calling for joint interposition of the states to get rid of those unconstitutional laws, was so widely regarded as a move for nullification that he had to fight that interpretation for the rest of his life. His great personal test, however, came in the War of 1812.

Throughout that conflict, the dominant political party in New England pursued a course that obstructed recruiting, hampered financing, flouted national authority, threatened secession, and gave more aid and comfort to the enemy than could have been furnished by a thousand overt traitors. Coupled with this was a campaign of personal vilification of the President unmatched in the country's annals. From all sides Madison received appeals to silence the seditious printers, preachers and politicians, either by law or through vigilante committees. To one such correspondent, the patriotic publicist Mathew Carey, Madison replied that "the wicked project of destroying the Union" was self-defeating: the great body of the people in New England could not be seduced from their loyalty. Carey did not agree. "The die is now cast," he wrote in the fall of 1814. "The Union will not last a year. Rapine and desolation and slaughter will lay everything waste." The whole blame for this lay on President Madison, who to all appeals "remained inflexible. As well might I have attempted to arrest the torrents of the Niagara as to prevail upon you."[33]

Peace came soon afterward with American fortunes rising. The Federalist party was crushed to death by the millstone of its own sedition. Upon Madison's retirement from the Presidency the citizens of Washington addressed him through a committee headed by the mayor in the following words:

Power and national glory, sir, have often before been acquired by the sword; but rarely without the sacrifice of civil or political liberty. . . . When we reflect that this sword was drawn under your guidance we cannot resist offering you our own as well as a nation's thanks for the vigilance with which you have restrained it within its proper limits, the energy with which you have directed it to its proper objects, and the safety with which you have wielded an armed force of fifty thousand men aided by an annual disbursement of many millions, without infringing a political, civil or religious right.[34]

The ensuing eight years are known in history as the Era of Good Feeling. They might with equal merit be called the first national dividend from the Madison Heritage.

3

THE BILL OF RIGHTS AND THE FEDERAL GOVERNMENT

Hugo L. Black

J AMES MADISON lived in the stirring times between 1750
   and 1836, during which the Colonies declared, fought for, and
won their independence from England. They then set up a new
national government dedicated to Liberty and Justice. Madison's
role in creating that government was such a major one that he
has since been generally referred to as the Father of our Constitution. He was a most influential member of the Philadelphia
Convention that submitted the Constitution to the people of the
states; he alone kept a comprehensive report of the daily proceedings of the Convention; he was an active member of the Virginia
Convention that adopted the Constitution after a bitter fight;
finally, as a member of the First Congress, he offered and sponsored through that body proposals that became the first ten
amendments, generally thought of as our Bill of Rights. For these
and many other reasons, Madison's words are an authentic source
to help us understand the Constitution and its Bill of Rights. In
the course of my discussion I shall have occasion to refer to some
of the many things Madison said about the meaning of the Constitution and the first ten amendments. In doing so, I shall refer
to statements made by him during the Bill of Rights debates
as reported in the *Annals of Congress*. There has been doubt
cast upon the accuracy of the reports of Congressional debates
and transactions in the *Annals*. I am assured by Mr. Irving Brant,
the eminent biographer of Madison, that Madison's discussions
of the Bill of Rights as reported in the *Annals* are shown to be
correct by Madison's own manuscripts on file in the Library of
Congress.[1]

What is a bill of rights? In the popular sense it is any document setting forth the liberties of the people. I prefer to think of
our Bill of Rights as including all provisions of the original Constitution and Amendments that protect individual liberty by
barring government from acting in a particular area or from acting
except under certain prescribed procedures. I have in mind such
clauses in the body of the Constitution itself as those which safe-

43

guard the right of habeas corpus, forbid bills of attainder and ex post facto laws, guarantee trial by jury, and strictly define treason and limit the way it can be tried and punished. I would certainly add to this list the last constitutional prohibition in Article Six that "no religious Test shall ever be required as a Qualification to any Office or public Trust under the United States."

I shall speak to you about the Bill of Rights only as it bears on powers of the Federal Government. Originally, the first ten amendments were not intended to apply to the states but, as the Supreme Court held in 1833 in *Barron v. Baltimore*,[2] were adopted to quiet fears extensively entertained that the powers of the big new national government "might be exercised in a manner dangerous to liberty." I believe that by virtue of the Fourteenth Amendment, the first ten amendments are now applicable to the states, a view I stated in *Adamson v. California*.[3] I adhere to that view. In this talk, however, I want to discuss only the extent to which the Bill of Rights limits the Federal Government.

In applying the Bill of Rights to the Federal Government there is today a sharp difference of views as to how far its provisions should be held to limit the lawmaking power of Congress. How this difference is finally resolved will, in my judgment, have far-reaching consequences upon our liberties. I shall first summarize what those different views are.

Some people regard the prohibitions of the Constitution, even its most unequivocal commands, as mere admonitions which Congress need not always observe. This viewpoint finds many different verbal expressions. For example, it is sometimes said that Congress may abridge a constitutional right if there is a clear and present danger that the free exercise of the right will bring about a substantive evil that Congress has authority to prevent. Or it is said that a right may be abridged where its exercise would cause so much injury to the public that this injury would outweigh the injury to the individual who is deprived of the right. Again, it is sometimes said that the Bill of Rights' guarantees must "compete" for survival against general powers expressly granted to Congress and that the individual's right must, if outweighed by the public interest, be subordinated to the Government's competing interest in denying the right. All of these formulations, and more with which you are doubtless familiar, rest, at least in part, on the premise that there are no "absolute" prohibitions in the Constitution, and that all constitutional problems are questions of reasonableness, proximity, and degree. This view comes close to the English doctrine of legislative omnipotence, qualified only by the possibility of a judicial veto if the Supreme Court finds that a congressional choice between "competing" policies has no reasonable basis.

I cannot accept this approach to the Bill of Rights. It is my belief that there *are* "absolutes" in our Bill of Rights, and that they were put there on purpose by men who knew what words meant, and meant their prohibitions to be "absolutes." The whole history and background of the Constitution and Bill of Rights, as I understand it, belies the assumption or conclusion that our ultimate constitutional freedoms are no more than our English ancestors had when they came to this new land to get new freedoms. The historical and practical purposes of a Bill of Rights, the very use of a written constitution, indigenous to America, the language the Framers used, the kind of three-department government they took pains to set up, all point to the creation of a government which was denied all power to do some things under any and all circumstances, and all power to do other things except precisely in the manner prescribed. In this talk I will state some of the reasons why I hold this view. In doing so, however, I shall not attempt to discuss the wholly different and complex problem of the marginal scope of each individual amendment as applied to the particular facts of particular cases. For example, there is a question as to whether the First Amendment was intended to protect speech that courts find "obscene." I shall not stress this or similar differences of construction, nor shall I add anything to the views I expressed in the recent case of *Smith v. California*.[4] I am primarily discussing here whether liberties *admittedly* covered by the Bill of Rights can nevertheless be abridged on the ground that a superior public interest justifies the abridgment. I think the Bill of Rights made its safeguards superior.

Today most Americans seem to have forgotten the ancient evils which forced their ancestors to flee to this new country and to form a government stripped of old powers used to oppress them. But the Americans who supported the Revolution and the adoption of our Constitution knew firsthand the dangers of tyrannical governments. They were familiar with the long existing practice of English persecutions of people wholly because of their religious or political beliefs. They knew that many accused of such offenses had stood, helpless to defend themselves, before biased legislators and judges.

John Lilburne, a Puritan dissenter, is a conspicuous example.[5] He found out the hard way that a citizen of England could not get a court and jury trial under English law if Parliament wanted to try and punish him in some kind of summary and unfair method of its own. Time and time again, when his religious or political activities resulted in criminal charges against him, he had demanded jury trials under the "law of the land" but had been refused. Due to "trials" either by Parliament, its legislative committees, or courts subservient to the King or to Parliament, against all of which he vigorously protested as contrary to "due process" or "the law of the land," Lilburne had been whipped, put in the pillory, sent to prison, heavily fined and banished from England, all its islands and dominions, under penalty of death should he return. This last sentence was imposed by a simple Act of Parliament without any semblance of a trial. Upon his defiant return he was arrested and subjected to an unfair trial for his life. His chief defense was that the Parliamentary conviction was a nullity, as a denial of "due process of law," which he claimed was guaranteed under Magna Carta, the 1628 Petition of Right, and statutes passed to carry them out. He also challenged the power of Parliament to enact bills of attainder on the same grounds—due process of law. Lilburne repeatedly and vehemently contended that he was entitled to notice, an indictment, and court trial by jury under the known laws of England; that he had a right to be represented by counsel; that he had a right to have witnesses summoned in his behalf and be confronted by the witnesses against him; that he could not be compelled to testify against himself. When Lilburne finally secured a jury, it courageously acquitted him, after which the jury itself was severely punished by the court.

Prompted largely by the desire to save Englishmen from such legislative mockeries of fair trials, Lilburne and others strongly advocated adoption of an "Agreement of the People" which contained most of the provisions of our present Bill of Rights. That Agreement would have done away with Parliamentary omnipotence. Lilburne pointed out that the basic defect of Magna Carta and statutes complementing it was that they were not binding on Parliament since "that which is done by one Parliament, as a Parliament, may be undone by the next Parliament: but an Agreement of the People begun and ended amongst the People can never come justly within the Parliament's cognizance to destroy."[6] The proposed "Agreement of the People," Lilburne argued, could be changed only by the people and would bind Parliament as the supreme "law of the land." This same idea was picked up before the adoption of our Federal Constitution by Massachusetts and New Hampshire, which adopted their constitutions only after popular referendums. Our Federal Constitution is largely attributable to the same current of thinking.

Unfortunately, our own colonial history also provided ample reasons for people to be afraid to vest too much power in the national government. There had been bills of attainder here; women had been convicted and sentenced to death as "witches"; Quakers, Baptists and various Protestant sects had been persecuted from time to time. Roger Williams left Massachusetts to breathe the

47

free air of new Rhode Island. Catholics were barred from holding office in many places. Test oaths were required in some of the colonies to bar any but Christians from holding office. In New England Quakers suffered death for their faith. Baptists were sent to jail in Virginia for preaching, which caused Madison, while a very young man, to deplore what he called that "diabolical hell-conceived principle of persecution."[7]

In the light of history, therefore, it is not surprising that when our Constitution was adopted without specific provisions to safeguard cherished individual rights from invasion by the legislative, as well as the executive and judicial departments of the National Government, a loud and irresistible clamor went up throughout the country. These protests were so strong that the Constitution was ratified by the very narrowest of votes in some of the states. It has been said, and I think correctly, that had there been no general agreement that a supplementary Bill of Rights would be adopted as soon as possible after Congress met, the Constitution would not have been ratified. It seems clear that this widespread demand for a Bill of Rights was due to a common fear of political and religious persecution should the national legislative power be left unrestrained as it was in England.

The form of government which was ordained and established in 1789 contains certain unique features which reflected the Framers' fear of arbitrary government and which clearly indicate an intention absolutely to limit what Congress could do. The first of these features is that our Constitution is written in a single document. Such constitutions are familiar today and it is not always remembered that our country was the first to have one. Certainly one purpose of a written constitution is to define and therefore more specifically limit government powers. An all-powerful government that can act as it pleases wants no such constitution —unless to fool the people. England had no written constitution and this once proved a source of tyranny, as our ancestors well knew. Jefferson said about this departure from the English type of government: "Our peculiar security is in the possession of a written Constitution. Let us not make it a blank paper by construction."[8]

A second unique feature of our Government is a Constitution supreme over the legislature. In England, statutes, Magna Carta and later declarations of rights had for centuries limited the power of the King, but they did not limit the power of Parliament. Although commonly referred to as a constitution, they were never the "supreme law of the land" in the way in which our Constitution is, much to the regret of statesmen like Pitt the elder. Parliament could change this English "Constitution"; Congress cannot change ours. Ours can only be changed by amendments ratified by three-fourths of the states. It was one of the great achievements of our Constitution that it ended legislative omnipotence here and placed all departments and agencies of government under one supreme law.

A third feature of our Government expressly designed to limit its powers was the division of authority into three coordinate branches none of which was to have supremacy over the others. This separation of powers with the checks and balances which each branch was given over the others was designed to prevent any branch, including the legislative, from infringing individual liberties safeguarded by the Constitution.

Finally, our Constitution was the first to provide a really independent judiciary. Moreover, as the Supreme Court held in *Marbury v. Madison*,[9] correctly I believe, this judiciary has the power to hold legislative enactments void that are repugnant to the Constitution and the Bill of Rights. In this country the judiciary was made independent because it has, I believe, the primary responsibility and duty of giving force and effect to constitutional liberties and limitations upon the executive and legislative branches. Judges in England were not always independent and they could not hold Parliamentary acts void. Consequently, English courts could not be counted on to protect the liberties of the people against invasion by the Parliament, as many unfortunate Englishmen found out, such as Sir Walter Raleigh, who was executed as the result of an unfair trial, and a lawyer named William Prynne, whose ears were first cut off by court order and who subsequently, by another court order, had his remaining ear stumps gouged out while he was on a pillory. Prynne's offenses were writing books and pamphlets.

All of the unique features of our Constitution show an underlying purpose to create a new kind of limited government. Central to all of the Framers of the Bill of Rights was the idea that since government, particularly the national government newly created, is a powerful institution, its officials—all of them—must be compelled to exercise their powers within strictly defined boundaries. As Madison told Congress, the Bill of Rights' limitations point "sometimes against the abuse of the Executive power, sometimes against the Legislative, and in some cases against the community itself; or, in other words, against the majority in favor of the minority."[10] Madison also explained that his proposed amendments were intended "to limit and qualify the powers of Government, by excepting out of the grant of power those cases in which the Government ought not to act, or to act only in a particular mode."[11] In the light of this purpose let us now turn to the language of the first ten amendments to consider whether their provisions were written as mere admonitions to Congress or as absolute commands, proceeding for convenience from the last to the first.

The last two Amendments, the Ninth and Tenth, are general in character, but both emphasize the limited nature of the Federal Government. Number Ten restricts federal power to what the Constitution delegates to the central government, reserving all other powers to the states or to the people. Number Nine attempts to make certain that enumeration of some rights must "not be construed to deny or disparage others retained by the people." The use of the words, "the people," in both these Amendments strongly emphasizes the desire of the Framers to protect individual liberty.

The Seventh Amendment states that "In Suits at common law, where the value in controversy shall exceed twenty dollars, the right of trial by jury shall be preserved . . ." This language clearly requires that jury trials must be afforded in the type of cases the Amendment describes. The Amendment goes on in equally un- equivocal words to command that "no fact tried by a jury, shall be otherwise re-examined in any Court of the United States, than according to the rules of the common law."

Amendments Five, Six, and Eight relate chiefly to the pro- cedures that government must follow when bringing its powers to bear against any person with a view to depriving him of his life, liberty, or property.

The Eighth Amendment forbids "excessive bail," "excessive fines," or the infliction of "cruel or unusual punishments." This is one of the less precise provisions. The courts are required to de- termine the meaning of such general terms as "excessive" and "unusual." But surely that does not mean that admittedly "exces- sive bail," "excessive fines," or "cruel punishments" could be justified on the ground of a "competing" public interest in carry- ing out some generally granted power like that given Congress to regulate commerce.

Amendment Six provides that in a criminal prosecution an ac- cused shall have a "speedy and public trial, by an impartial jury of the State and district wherein the crime shall have been com- mitted, which district shall have been previously ascertained by law, and to be informed of the nature and cause of the accusa- tion; to be confronted with the witnesses against him; to have compulsory process for obtaining witnesses in his favor, and have the Assistance of Counsel for his defence." All of these require- ments are cast in terms both definite and absolute. Trial by jury was also guaranteed in the original Constitution. The additions here, doubtless prompted by English trials of Americans away from their homes, are that a trial must be "speedy and public," "by an impartial jury," and in a district which "shall have been previously ascertained by law." If there is any one thing that is certain it is that the Framers intended both in the original Constitution and in the Sixth Amendment that persons charged with crime by the Federal Government have a right to be tried by jury. Suppose juries began acquitting people Congress thought should be convicted. Could Congress then provide some other form of trial, say by an administrative agency, or the military, where convictions could be more readily and certainly obtained, if it thought the safety of the nation so required? How about secret trials? By *partial* juries? Can it be that these are not absolute prohibitions?

The Sixth Amendment requires notice of the cause of an accusation, confrontation by witnesses, compulsory process and assistance of counsel. The experience of centuries has demonstrated the value of these procedures to one on trial for crime. And this Amendment purports to guarantee them by clear language. But if there are no absolutes in the Bill of Rights, these guarantees too can be taken away by Congress on findings that a competing public interest requires that defendants be tried without notice, without witnesses, without confrontation, and without counsel.

The Fifth Amendment provides:

No person shall be held to answer for a capital, or otherwise infamous crime, unless on a presentment or indictment of a Grand Jury, except in cases arising in the land or naval forces, or in the Militia, when in actual service in time of War or public danger; nor shall any person be subject for the same offence to be twice put in jeopardy of life or limb; nor shall be compelled in any criminal case to be a witness against himself, nor be deprived of life, liberty, or property, without due process of law; nor shall private property be taken for public use, without just compensation.

Most of these Fifth Amendment prohibitions are both definite and unequivocal. There has been much controversy about the meaning of "due process of law." Whatever its meaning, however, there can be no doubt that it must be granted. Moreover, few doubt that it has an historical meaning which denies Government the right to take away life, liberty, or property without trials properly conducted according to the Constitution and laws validly made in accordance with it. This, at least, was the meaning of "due process of law" when used in Magna Carta and other old English Statutes where it was referred to as "the law of the land."

The Fourth Amendment provides:

The right of the people to be secure in their persons, houses, papers, and effects, against unreasonable searches and seizures, shall not be violated, and no Warrants shall issue, but upon probable cause, supported by Oath or affirmation, and particularly describing the place to be searched, and the persons or things to be seized.

The use of the word "unreasonable" in this Amendment means, of course, that not *all* searches and seizures are prohibited. Only those which are *unreasonable* are unlawful. There may be much difference of opinion about whether a particular search or seizure is unreasonable and therefore forbidden by this Amendment. But if it *is* unreasonable, it is absolutely prohibited.

Likewise, the provision which forbids warrants for arrest, search or seizure without "probable cause" is itself an absolute prohibition.

The Third Amendment provides that:

No Soldier shall, in time of peace be quartered in any house, without the consent of the Owner, nor in time of war, but in a manner to be prescribed by law.

Americans had recently suffered from the quartering of British troops in their homes, and so this Amendment is written in language that apparently no one has ever thought could be violated on the basis of an overweighing public interest.

Amendment Two provides that:

A well regulated Militia, being necessary to the security of a free State, the right of the people to keep and bear Arms, shall not be infringed.

Although the Supreme Court has held this Amendment to include only arms necessary to a well-regulated militia, as so construed, its prohibition is absolute.

This brings us to the First Amendment. It reads:

Congress shall make no law respecting an establishment of religion, or prohibiting the free exercise thereof; or abridging the freedom of speech, or of the press; or the right of the people peaceably to assemble, and to petition the Government for a redress of grievances.

The phrase "Congress shall make no law" is composed of plain words, easily understood. The Framers knew this. The language used by Madison in his proposal was different, but no less emphatic and unequivocal. That proposal is worth reading:

The civil rights of none shall be abridged on account of religious belief or worship, nor shall any national religion be established, nor shall the full and equal rights of conscience be in any manner, or on any pretext, infringed.
The people shall not be deprived or abridged of their right to speak, to write, or to publish their sentiments; and the freedom of the press, as one of the great bulwarks of liberty, shall be inviolable.
The people shall not be restrained from peaceably assembling and consulting for their common good; nor from applying to the Legislature by petitions, or remonstrances, for redress of their grievances.[12]

Neither as offered nor as adopted is the language of this Amendment anything less than absolute. Madison was emphatic about this. He told the Congress that under it "The right of freedom of speech is secured; the liberty of the press is expressly declared to be *beyond the reach of this Government* . . ."[13] (Emphasis added in all quotations.) Some years later Madison wrote that "it would seem scarcely possible to doubt that *no power whatever* over the press was supposed to be delegated by the Constitution, as it originally stood, and that the amendment was intended as a *positive and absolute reservation of it.*"[14] With reference to the positive nature of the First Amendment's command against infringement of religious liberty, Madison later said that "there is not a shadow of right in the general government to intermeddle with religion,"[15] and that "this subject is, for the honor of America, perfectly free and unshackled. The *government has no jurisdiction over it.*"[16]

To my way of thinking, at least, the history and language of the Constitution and the Bill of Rights, which I have discussed with you, make it plain that one of the primary purposes of the Constitution with its amendments was to withdraw from the Government all power to act in certain areas—whatever the scope of those areas may be. If I am right in this then there is, at least in those areas, no justification whatever for "balancing" a particular right against some expressly granted power of Congress. If the Constitution withdraws from Government all power over subject matter in an area, such as religion, speech, press, assembly, and petition, there is nothing over which authority may be exerted.

The Framers were well aware that the individual rights they sought to protect might be easily nullified if subordinated to the general powers granted to Congress. One of the reasons for adoption of the Bill of Rights was to prevent just that. Specifically the people feared that the "necessary and proper" clause could be used to project the generally granted Congressional powers into the protected areas of individual rights. One need only read the debates in the various states to find out that this is true. But if these debates leave any doubt, Mr. Madison's words to Congress should remove it. In speaking of the "necessary and proper" clause and its possible effect on freedom of religion he said, as reported in the *Annals of Congress:*

Whether the words are necessary or not, he did not mean to say, but they had been required by some of the State Conventions, who seemed to entertain an opinion that under the clause of the Constitution, which gave power to Congress to make all laws *necessary and proper* to carry into execution the Constitution, and the laws made under it, enabled them to make laws of such a nature as might infringe the rights of conscience, and establish a national religion; to prevent these effects he presumed the amendment was intended, and he thought it as well expressed as the nature of the language would admit.[17]

It seems obvious to me that Congress, in exercising its general powers, is expressly forbidden to use means prohibited by the Bill of Rights. Whatever else the phrase "necessary and proper" may mean, it must be that Congress may only adopt such means to carry out its powers as are "proper," that is, not specifically prohibited.

It has also been argued that since freedom of speech, press, and religion in England were narrow freedoms at best, and since there were many English laws infringing those freedoms, our First Amendment should not be thought to bar similar infringements by Congress. Again one needs only to look to the debates in Congress over the First Amendment to find that the First Amendment cannot be treated as a mere codification of English law. Mr. Madison made a clear explanation to Congress that it was the purpose of the First Amendment to grant greater protection than England afforded its citizens. He said:

In the declaration of rights which that country has established, the truth is, they have gone no farther than to raise a barrier against the power of the Crown; the power of the Legislature is left altogether indefinite. Although I know whenever the great rights, the trial by jury, freedom of the press, or liberty of conscience, come in question in that body, the invasion of them is resisted by able advocates, yet their Magna Charta does not contain any one provision for the security of those rights, respecting which the people of America are most alarmed. The freedom of the press and rights of conscience, those choicest privileges of the people, are unguarded in the British Constitution.

But although the case may be widely different, and it may not be thought necessary to provide limits for the legislative power in that country, yet a different opinion prevails in the United States.[18]

It was the desire to give the people of America greater protection against the powerful Federal Government than the English had had against their government that caused the Framers to put these freedoms of expression, again in the words of Madison, "beyond the reach of this Government."

When closely analyzed the idea that there can be no "absolute" constitutional guarantees in the Bill of Rights is frightening to contemplate even as to individual safeguards in the original Constitution. Take, for instance, the last clause in Article Six that "no religious Test shall ever be required" for a person to hold office in the United States. Suppose Congress should find that some religious sect was dangerous because of its foreign affiliations. Such was the belief on which English test oaths rested for a long time and some of the states had test oaths on that assumption at the time, and after, our Constitution was adopted in 1789. Could Congress, or the Supreme Court, or both, put this precious privilege to be free from test oaths on scales, find it outweighed by some other public interest, and therefore make United States officials and employees swear they did not and never had belonged to or associated with a particular religious group suspected of disloyalty? Can Congress, in the name of overbalancing necessity, suspend habeas corpus in peacetime? Are there circumstances under which Congress could, after nothing more than a legislative bill of attainder, take away a man's life, liberty, or property? Hostility of the Framers toward bills of attainder was so great that they took the unusual step of barring such legislative punishments by the States as well as the Federal Government. They wanted to remove any possibility of such proceedings anywhere in this country. This is not strange in view of the fact that they were much closer than we are to the great Act of Attainder by the Irish Parliament, in 1688, which condemned between two and three thousand men, women, and children to exile or death without anything that even resembled a trial.[19]

Perhaps I can show you the consequences of the balancing approach to the Bill of Rights liberties by a practical demonstration of how it might work. The last clause of the Fifth Amendment is: "nor shall private property be taken for public use, without just compensation." On its face this command looks absolute, but if one believes that it should be weighed against the powers granted to Congress, there might be some circumstances in which this right would have to give way, just as there are some circumstances in which it is said the right of freedom of religion, speech, press, assembly and petition can be balanced away. Let us see how the balancing concept would apply to the just compensation provision of the Bill of Rights in the following wholly imaginary judicial opinion of Judge X:

This case presents an important question of constitutional law. The United States is engaged in a stupendous national defense undertaking which requires the acquisition of much valuable land throughout the country. The plaintiff here owns 500 acres of land. The location of the land gives it a peculiarly strategic value for carrying out the defense program. Due to the great national emergency that exists, Congress concluded that the United States could not afford at this time to pay compensation for the lands which it needed to acquire. For this reason an act was passed authorizing seizure without compensation of all the lands required for the defense establishment.

In reaching a judgment on this case, I cannot shut my eyes to the fact that the United States is in a desperate condition at this time. Nor can I, under established canons of constitutional construction, invalidate a Congressional enactment if there are any rational grounds upon which Congress could have passed it. I think there are such grounds here. Highly important among the powers granted Congress by the Constitution are the powers to declare war, maintain a navy, and raise and support armies. This, of course, means the power to conduct war successfully. To make sure that Congress is not unduly restricted in the exercise of these constitutional powers, the Constitution also gives Congress power to make all laws 'necessary and proper to carry into execution the foregoing powers . . .' This 'necessary and proper' clause applies to the powers to make war and support armies as it does to all the other granted powers.

Plaintiff contends, however, that the Fifth Amendment's provision about compensation is so absolute a command that Congress is wholly without authority to violate it, however great this nation's emergency and peril may be. I must reject this contention. We must never forget that it is a constitution we are expounding. And a constitution, unlike ordinary statutes, must endure for ages; it must be adapted to changing conditions and the needs of changing communities. Without such capacity for change, our Constitution would soon be outmoded and become a dead letter. Therefore its words must never be read as rigid absolutes. The Bill of Rights' commands, no more than any others, can stay the hands of Congress from doing that which the general welfare imperatively demands. When two great constitutional provisions like these conflict—as here the power to make war conflicts with the requirements for just compensation— it becomes the duty of courts to weigh the constitutional right of an individual to compensation against the power of Congress to wage a successful war.

While the question is not without doubt, I have no hesitation in finding the challenged Congressional act valid. Driven by the absolute necessity to protect the nation from foreign aggression, the national debt has risen to billions of dollars. The Government's credit is such that interest rates have soared. Under these circumstances, Congress was rationally entitled to find that if it paid for all the lands it needs it might bankrupt the nation and render it helpless in its hour of greatest need. Weighing as I must the loss the individual will suffer because he has to surrender his land to the nation without compensation against the great public interest in conducting war, I hold the act valid. A decree will be entered accordingly.

Of course, I would not decide this case this way nor do I think any other judge would so decide it today. My reason for refusing this approach would be that I think the Fifth Amendment's command is absolute and not to be overcome without constitutional amendment even in times of grave emergency. But I think this wholly fictitious opinion fairly illustrates the possibilities of the balancing approach, not only as to the just compensation clause, but as to other provisions of the Bill of Rights as well. The great danger of the judiciary balancing process is that in times of emergency and stress it gives Government the power to do what it thinks necessary to protect itself, regardless of the rights of individuals. If the need is great, the right of Government can always be said to outweigh the rights of the individual. If "balancing" is accepted as the test, it would be hard for any conscientious judge to hold otherwise in times of dire need. And laws adopted in times of dire need are often very hasty and oppressive laws, especially when, as often happens, they are carried over and accepted as normal. Furthermore, the balancing approach to basic individual liberties assumes to legislators and judges more power than either the Framers or I myself believe should be entrusted, without limitation, to any man or any group of men.

It seems to me that the "balancing" approach also disregards all of the unique features of our Constitution which I described earlier. In reality this approach returns us to the state of legislative supremacy which existed in England and which the Framers were so determined to change once and for all. On the one hand, it denies the judiciary its constitutional power to measure acts of Congress by the standards set down in the Bill of Rights. On the other hand, though apparently reducing judicial powers by saying that acts of Congress may be held unconstitutional only when they are found to have no rational legislative basis, this approach really gives the Court, along with Congress, a greater power, that of overriding the plain commands of the Bill of Rights on a finding of weighty public interest. In effect, it changes the direction of our form of government from a government of limited powers to a government in which Congress may do anything that courts believe to be "reasonable."

Of course the decision to provide a constitutional safeguard for a particular right, such as the fair trial requirements of the Fifth and Sixth Amendments and the right of free speech protection of the First, involves a balancing of conflicting interests. Strict procedures may release guilty men; protecting speech and press may involve dangers to a particular government. I believe, however, that the Framers themselves did this balancing when they wrote the Constitution and the Bill of Rights. They appreciated the risks involved and they decided that certain rights should be guaranteed regardless of these risks. Courts have neither the right nor the power to review this original decision of the Framers and to attempt to make a different evaluation of the importance of the rights granted in the Constitution. Where conflicting values exist in the field of individual liberties protected by the Constitution, that document settles the conflict, and its policy should not be changed without constitutional amendments by the people in the manner provided by the people.

Misuse of government power, particularly in times of stress, has brought suffering to humanity in all ages about which we have authentic history. Some of the world's noblest and finest men have suffered ignominy and death for no crime—unless unorthodoxy is a crime. Even enlightened Athens had its victims such as Socrates. Because of the same kind of bigotry, Jesus, the great Dissenter, was put to death on a wooden cross. The flames of inquisitions all over the world have warned that men endowed with unlimited government power, even earnest men, consecrated to a cause, are dangerous.

For my own part, I believe that our Constitution, with its absolute guarantees of individual rights, is the best hope for the aspirations of freedom which men share everywhere. I cannot agree with those who think of the Bill of Rights as an 18th century straitjacket, unsuited for this age. It is old but not all old things are bad. The evils it guards against are not only old, they are with us now, they exist today. Almost any morning you open your daily paper you can see where some person somewhere in the world is on trial or has just been convicted of supposed disloyalty to a new group controlling the government which has set out to purge its suspected enemies and all those who had dared to be against its successful march to power. Nearly always you see that these political heretics are being tried by military tribunals or some other summary and sure method for disposition of the accused. Now and then we even see the convicted victims as they march to their execution.

Experience all over the world has demonstrated, I fear, that the distance between stable, orderly government and one that has been taken over by force is not so great as we have assumed. Our own free system to live and progress has to have intelligent citizens, citizens who cannot only think and speak and write to influence people, but citizens who are free to do that without fear of governmental censorship or reprisal.

The provisions of the Bill of Rights that safeguard fair legal procedures came about largely to protect the weak and the oppressed from punishment by the strong and the powerful who wanted to stifle the voices of discontent raised in protest against oppression and injustice in public affairs. Nothing that I have read in the Congressional debates on the Bill of Rights indicates that there was any belief that the First Amendment contained any qualifications. The only arguments that tended to look in this direction at all were those that said "that all paper barriers against the power of the community are too weak to be worthy of attention."[20] Suggestions were also made in and out of Congress that a Bill of Rights would be a futile gesture since there would be no way to enforce the safeguards for freedom it provided. Mr. Madison answered this argument in these words:

If they [the Bill of Rights amendments] are incorporated into the Constitution, independent tribunals of justice will consider themselves in a peculiar manner the guardians of those rights; they will be an impenetrable bulwark against any assumption of power in the Legislative or Executive; they will be naturally led to resist every encroachment upon rights expressly stipulated for in the Constitution by the declaration of rights.[21]

I fail to see how courts can escape this sacred trust.

Since the earliest days philosophers have dreamed of a country where the mind and spirit of man would be free; where there would be no limits to inquiry; where men would be free to explore the unknown and to challenge the most deeply rooted beliefs and principles. Our First Amendment was a bold effort to adopt this principle—to establish a country with no legal restrictions of any kind upon the subjects people could investigate, discuss and deny. The Framers knew, better perhaps than we do today, the risks they were taking. They knew that free speech might be the friend of change and revolution. But they also knew that it is always the deadliest enemy of tyranny. With this knowledge they still believed that the ultimate happiness and security of a nation lies in its ability to explore, to change, to grow and ceaselessly to adapt itself to new knowledge born of inquiry free from any kind of governmental control over the mind and spirit of man. Loyalty comes from love of good government, not fear of a bad one.

The First Amendment is truly the heart of the Bill of Rights. The Framers balanced its freedoms of religion, speech, press, assembly and petition against the needs of a powerful central government, and decided that in those freedoms lies this nation's only true security. They were not afraid for men to be free. We should not be. We should be as confident as Jefferson was when he said in his First Inaugural Address:

If there be any among us who would wish to dissolve this Union or to change its republican form, let them stand undisturbed as monuments of the safety with which error of opinion may be tolerated where reason is left free to combat it.[22]

4

THE BILL OF RIGHTS AND THE STATES

William J. Brennan, Jr.

I AM deeply conscious of the honor of standing at this podium to deliver one of the lectures which, in James Madison's name, review the safeguards of liberty which he did so much to weave into our constitutional fabric. We owe a great debt to every Framer without exception. But we justly reserve for Madison alone the title of Father of the Constitution. It was he who drafted the Virginia plan which became the framework for the Constitution of the United States. It was he whose inspired leadership gave us the Bill of Rights.

These remarks will discuss the application of the Bill of Rights to the states. The seeds of that controversial subject were sown before the nation was formed. When the Declaration of Independence severed the tie that bound the colonies to the Throne of England, each colony fell back upon its own inherent sovereignty, and the people of each, with the exceptions at first of Connecticut and Rhode Island, formed for themselves a constitution, local, separate, and apart. Each state, formerly a colony, took fierce pride in its separate sovereignty. The states formed a Confederation, but so jealous was each of its sovereign prerogatives that too few powers essential to union were surrendered, and the enterprise foundered.

The constitutions of the original states anticipated the national Constitution in declaring the doctrine that there are human liberties which are inalienable. This doctrine has ever since been the center and core of the American idea of limited government. The government of each state was the creation of the people of the state; the source of power was the people of that state. The only end and aim of government was to secure the people in their natural and civil rights. However, union under the Articles of Confederation, and later under the Constitution, was not effected by the people as a mass, but by the several peoples of the several states. In other words, the nation was created by the states and the people of the states, and not by the people separate from the states. The states remained possessed of very power of sovereignty which

67

the several peoples of the several states had not delegated to the United States. This feature was basic to both the Articles of Confederation and to the Constitution. A purpose of the Constitution was to improve upon the Articles of Confederation, and "to form a more perfect union" of states. The Framers' aim was to grant the national government only such powers of sovereignty as were necessary to attain ends better secured by a national government than by the states individually or in confederation. Powers of sovereignty as they affected only a state and the people of the state were reserved to the state. "The powers reserved to the several States," said Madison, "will extend to all the objects which, in the ordinary course of affairs, concern the lives, liberties, and properties of the people, and the internal order, improvement, and prosperity of the State."[1]

In contrast, the national government might exercise only the powers enumerated in the Constitution, together with the power to make all laws necessary and proper for carrying into execution the enumerated powers. Even these limitations were not enough for the peoples of some of the states. So widespread was the fear that the national government might encroach upon the sovereignty of the states, and the sovereign rights of the peoples of the several states, that a number of states were reluctant to ratify the new Constitution without an express limitation on the authority of the national government to exercise certain powers. This was the genesis of the Bill of Rights.

It is natural then that the first ten amendments should have been conceived only as a bulwark to the states, and the peoples of the states, against encroachments of the national government upon the sovereignty which the people of each state reserved to themselves and to their state government. Protection against encroachment on individual rights by a state government was a matter for the state constitution. This division of sovereign powers between the states and the nation gave us, said John Quincy Adams, "the most complicated government on the face of the globe."[2]

The proper preservation of that division constituted from the beginning, and constitutes still, an important value in every consideration of the application of the Federal Bill of Rights to the states. It is from this division that the concepts derive which we call "states' rights" or "the demands of our federalism." For "it may be not unreasonably said that the preservation of the States, and the maintenance of their governments, are as much within the design and care of the Constitution as the preservation of the Union and the maintenance of the National government."[3]

Yet there was support for the inclusion in the Constitution of restraints against encroachment by state governments upon rights of the peoples of the several states. Indeed, the Framers did include some restraints of this nature in the body of the Constitution itself. The prohibitions in article I, section 10, which forbid every state to pass any bill of attainder or ex post facto law or law impairing the obligation of contracts, are examples. Madison himself wanted more such restraints in the Constitution. He was by no means happy with the bills of rights which at that time were in the state constitutions. Said he: "[S]ome States have no bills of rights [four states had none], there are others provided with very defective ones, and there are others whose bills of rights are not only defective, but absolutely improper; instead of securing some in the full extent which republican principles would require, they limit them too much to agree with the common ideas of liberty."[4]

Madison proposed not ten, but, in the form the House sent them to the Senate, seventeen amendments. The House and Senate finally agreed on twelve to be submitted to the states. Only the last ten of the twelve were ratified to become the first ten amendments. Among the proposals which the Senate rejected was Number XIV of the seventeen submitted by the House. Number XIV —a number prophetic of things to come seventy-nine years later— read: "No State shall infringe the right of trial by Jury in criminal cases, nor the rights of conscience, nor the freedom of speech, or of the press."[5] Madison thought that these restrictions on state power were "of equal, if not greater importance than those already made"[6] in article I, section 10. There was, he said, "more danger of those powers being abused by the State Governments than by the Government of the United States."[7] Indeed, he "conceived this to be the most valuable amendment in the whole list. If there were any reason to restrain the Government of the United States from infringing upon these essential rights, it was equally necessary that they should be secured against the State Governments."[8] It is only conjecture that Number XIV was defeated in the Senate by the votes of states whose systems of established churches would have been outlawed under this proposal. Some states (Massachusetts until 1833) maintained established churches long after the First Amendment became effective.

Plainly enough, however, Madison had no thought that any of the first eight amendments which were adopted extended to the states. Yet as early as 1825, a textbook, the work of William Rawle, a Philadelphia lawyer who had served as United States Attorney, argued that except for the First and Seventh Amendments, the guarantees of the Bill of Rights

form parts of the declared rights of the people, of which neither the state powers nor those of the Union can ever deprive them. . . . A declaration of rights . . . equalizes all and binds all. It becomes part of the general compact. Each state is obliged while it remains a member of the Union, to preserve the republican form of government in all its purity and all its strength. The people of each state, by the amended constitution, pledge themselves to each other for the sacred preservation of certain detailed principles, without which the republican form of government would be impure and weak.[9]

Rawle's mistake was in conceiving that "We the people" in the Preamble meant that the Constitution was the creation of the American people compounded into one common mass; the Constitution was in fact the creation of states and of people within each of the states.

Eight years later, in 1833, the Supreme Court made this clear in *Barron v. Baltimore*,[10] the first case to present the question of the application of a provision of the Bill of Rights to a state. The City of Baltimore made street improvements which destroyed the commercial use of a wharf. The owner of the wharf sought damages from the city. The Maryland Court of Appeals held that he was not entitled to any. The wharf owner contended in the United States Supreme Court that the Maryland judgment violated the provision of the Fifth Amendment, "nor shall private property be taken for public use, without just compensation." That provision, the owner argued, "being in favor of the liberty of the citizen, ought to be so construed as to restrain the legislative power of a state, as well as that of the United States."[11] Marshall thought the argument was "not of much difficulty." The Bill of Rights, he said, did not operate against state, but only federal power. The Federal Constitution, Marshall went on,

was ordained and established by the people of the United States for themselves, for their own government, and not for the government of the individual states. Each state established a constitution for itself, and, in that constitution, provided such limitations and restrictions on the powers of its particular government, as its judgment dictated. The people of the United States framed such a government for the United States as they supposed best adapted to their situation and best calculated to promote their interests. The powers they conferred on this government were to be exercised by itself; and the limitations on power, if expressed in general terms, are naturally, and, we think, necessarily, applicable to the government created by the instrument. They are limitations of power granted in the instrument itself; not of distinct governments, framed by different persons and for different purposes.[12]

The Court reaffirmed this proposition in a number of cases decided over the next twenty-five years.[13]

Each of the states in time adopted a bill of rights. Many of these followed the federal pattern. From all that appears, until the Civil War, they bore out Madison's prophesy that "if once bills of rights are established in all the States as well as the Federal

Constitution, we shall find that, although some of them are rather unimportant, yet, upon the whole, they will have a salutary tendency."[14]

It was after the Civil War that the demand arose for national protection against alleged abuses of state power. It was charged that the former Confederate states denied freedmen the protections for life, liberty, and property accorded the white man under state constitutions and laws. The constitutionality of remedial legislation passed by Congress was thought to be doubtful. This doubt led to the proposal for a constitutional amendment to remove any question of congressional power. This amendment became the Fourteenth Amendment.

Deep passions and extreme partisanship marked the controversy in and out of Congress over the adoption of the Fourteenth Amendment. It was the "Age of Hate in American politics."[15] The opponents' most powerful argument, repeated and repeated in the debates in Congress and up and down the land, was that the grant of powers under the amendment would mean that the sovereign powers reserved to the states, the keystone of the structure erected by the Framers, would be transferred to the national government. Senator Browning of Illinois said:

If the proposed amendments of the Constitution be adopted, new and enormous power will be claimed and exercised by Congress, as warranted by such amendments, and the whole structure of our Government will perhaps gradually but yet surely be revolutionized. And so with the Judiciary. If the proposed amendments be adopted, they may and certainly will be used substantially to annihilate the State judiciaries. . . . Be assured, if this new provision be engrafted in the Constitution, it will, in time, change the entire texture and structure of our Government, and sweep away all the guarantees of safety devised and provided by our patriotic sires of the revolution. . . .[16]

This argument was not without force when directed to the first section of the amendment as originally proposed. That proposal read: "Congress shall have power to make all laws which shall be necessary and proper to secure to citizens of each State all privileges and immunities of citizens in the several States . . . and to all persons in the several States equal protection in the rights of life, liberty and property. . . ."[17] This certainly sounded like an affirmative grant of power to the Congress to supersede state laws. This version, however, never got beyond committee. There was quickly substituted the language now in the first section of the amendment, "No state shall make or enforce any law which shall abridge the privileges or immunities of citizens of the United States; nor shall any state deprive any person of life, liberty or property without due process of law; nor deny to any person within its jurisdiction the equal protection of the laws." That language, like the language of Article I, Section 10 of the Constitution, is language of limitation. On its face it appears simply to impose limits upon, and not to authorize Congress to displace, the states in the exercise of their traditional authority to legislate directly upon all their citizens in regard to life, liberty, and property. But section 5 of the amendment does grant the Congress affirmative authority to enforce these prohibitions by appropriate legislation. The substituted provision in no wise stilled the cries that the amendment would effect a disruption of the historic distribution of sovereign powers and bring an end to the noble plan of the Framers. The opponents could not prevent the adoption of the amendment. But it cannot be said that they were completely vanquished. For events were to prove that the Supreme Court would interpret the amendment in a way which would go far to relieve their worry that its restraints effected the loss of separate and independent autonomy to the states.

The first case that came to the Court did not present the question of the application of a specific guarantee of the Federal Bill of Rights to the states. It is an interesting conjecture whether state power would have been vindicated had such been the case. The first decision, known as the *Slaughter-House Cases*,[18] came down in 1872. There was involved the constitutionality of a Louisiana statute which put certain New Orleans butchers out of business by conferring on a single corporation a monopoly of the business of slaughtering cattle. The affected butchers claimed that they were denied one of the "privileges or immunities of citizens of the United States" protected from abridgment by the states under the Amendment.

There is much evidence that those who coined the phrase the "privileges or immunities of citizens of the United States" were not certain what privileges and immunities were covered by these words. The Court held by a five-to-four vote that whatever privileges or immunities were included, the privilege of following the butcher calling in the State of Louisiana was not one of them. The privilege of following that calling was a privilege not of United States citizenship, but of state citizenship, and the prohibition of the calling by Louisiana was therefore inoffensive to the prohibition of the Fourteenth Amendment.

Nothing in the words themselves compelled that conclusion. Many still believe that the dissenting opinion in the *Slaughter-House Cases* expressed the sounder view. The Court was later to acknowledge that "Criticism of . . . [the *Slaughter-House Cases*] has never entirely ceased, nor has it ever received universal assent by members of this court. Undoubtedly, it gave much less effect to the Fourteenth Amendment than some of the public men active in framing it intended, and disappointed many others."[19] But the prevailing opinion frankly disclosed the basic concern of the Justices who subscribed to it. To embrace, among "the privileges or immunities of citizens of the United States," the privilege of a Louisiana citizen to follow the butcher's trade, would be, the Court declared,

to transfer the security and protection of all the civil rights . . . to the Federal government[,] . . . to bring within the power of Congress the entire domain of civil rights heretofore belonging exclusively to the States [.] . . .

74

[The effect of] so great a departure from the structure and spirit of our institutions . . . is to fetter and degrade the State governments by subjecting them to the control of Congress, in the exercise of powers heretofore universally conceded to them of the most ordinary and fundamental character. . . .

We are convinced that no such results were intended by the Congress . . . nor by the legislatures . . . which ratified . . . [this amendment].[20]

But what of the privileges and immunities declared in the Federal Bill of Rights? Might not they be considered the logical referent of "privileges or immunities of citizens of the United States," since they are expressly declared in the United States Constitution itself? The Supreme Court was soon to reject that interpretation.

In case after case, beginning in 1875—each case presenting the question as to a different guarantee[21]—the Court held that the guarantees in the Federal Bill of Rights were not among "the privileges or immunities of citizens of the United States." The process was completed in a series of cases decided from 1887 to 1908 in which the Court time after time rejected efforts to persuade it that the federal list of rights in its entirety came within the protected privileges or immunities.[22]

I should complete here the story of the so-called "incorporation theory"—that is, the theory that the Fourteenth Amendment was intended to make all of the Federal Bill of Rights applicable to the states. This view had the strong support of the first Justice Harlan, of Mr. Justice Brewer, and of Mr. Justice Field as early as 1892.[23] It was espoused in 1947 by Mr. Justice Black in his famous dissent in *Adamson v. California*.[24] Mr. Justice Black believes that in the earlier cases the Court fell into error in failing sufficiently to consult the history of the Fourteenth Amendment. He reads that history as demonstrating that the Framers of the Fourteenth Amendment intended to enfold the Federal Bill of Rights within its commands.

My study of the historical events that culminated in the Fourteenth Amendment, and the expressions of those who sponsored and favored, as well as those who opposed its submission and passage, persuades me that one of the chief objects that the provisions of the Amendment's first section, separately, and as a whole, were intended to accomplish was to make the Bill of Rights, applicable to the states. With full knowledge of the import of the *Barron* decision, the framers and backers of the Fourteenth Amendment proclaimed its purpose to be to overturn the constitutional rule that case had announced.[25]

Three other Justices shared this view with Mr. Justice Black in 1947,[26] but it has yet to command the support of a majority of the Court.

However, the rejection of the incorporation theory, and the disregard of the privileges and immunities clause, have not closed every door in the Fourteenth Amendment against the application of the Federal Bill of Rights to the states. The Court has opened a door through the Fourteenth Amendment's due process clause. During the last half century the Court has opened that door to admit some of the federal list. Moreover, the Court has indicated that the door may be opened to still more. True, it is often insisted that the application to the states of a safeguard embodied in the first eight amendments is not made "because those rights are enumerated in the first eight Amendments, but because they are of such a nature that they are included in the conception of due process of law."[27] In other words, the insistence is that the due process clause is infused with "an independent potency" not resting upon the Bill of Rights.[28] With all respect, I think that Mr. Justice Cardozo's analysis is more accurate. In 1937, he described what the Court has done as a process by which the guarantees "have been taken over from the earlier articles of the federal bill of rights and brought within the Fourteenth Amendment by a *process of absorption. . . . [T] he process of absorption* has had its source in the belief that neither liberty nor justice would exist if . . . [those guarantees] were sacrificed."[29] The criteria by which judgments have been made in the past as to which specifics should be absorbed, and which not, are neither precise nor definitive. The Court early said: "Few phrases of the law are so elusive of exact apprehension as . . . [due process of law]. . . . This court has always declined to give a comprehensive definition of it, and has preferred that its full meaning should be gradually ascertained by the process of inclusion and exclusion in the course of the decisions of cases as they arise."[30]

The considerations of federalism of course loom large. A decision rejecting absorption of a particular guarantee will usually be made to rest on the inconsistency of its absorption with "the full power of the State to order its own affairs and govern its own people."[31] Where this consideration has been overborne, and the absorption of some specific has been decreed, the Court has said of that specific that it is "of the very essence of a scheme of ordered liberty,"[32] or that it is included among "those fundamental principles of liberty and justice which lie at the base of all our civil and political institutions,"[33] or that it is among those personal immunities "so rooted in the traditions and conscience of our people as to be ranked as fundamental."[34]

How many of the specifics of the Bill of Rights have been held to be absorbed by the Fourteenth Amendment? We start with the First Amendment.

By one or more of the tests all of the protections of the First Amendment have been held to extend to the exercise of state power. This development has taken place in a series of decisions handed down over the last thirty-five years. As recently as 1922, in *Prudential Insurance Co. v. Cheek*,[35] the Court had held that the Fourteenth Amendment did not make the protections of the First Amendment binding on the states. Since 1925, however, decisions have extended against state power the amendment's protections for religion, speech, press, assembly, and petition.[36] Of freedom of thought and speech, said Mr. Justice Cardozo, "one may say that it is the matrix, the indispensable condition, of nearly every other

77

form of freedom."[37] Occasionally a member of the Court has suggested that the freedom of speech and of the press may be secured by the Fourteenth Amendment less broadly than it is secured by the First,[38] but this view has never persuaded even a substantial minority of the Court.

The First Amendment's protections for the cherished rights of mind and spirit thus stand guard against both state and federal governments. Voices are heard, however, which insist that these protections have not been as vigorously enforced against either federal or state power as they should be—that the judiciary, as to First Amendment rights particularly, have not justified Madison's faith that "independent tribunals of justice will consider themselves in a peculiar manner the guardians of those rights."[39] Last year my colleague, Mr. Justice Black, opened these lectures with his distinguished paper on the subject whether the guarantees of the Bill of Rights, or at least most of them, are "absolutes" which strictly limit the exercise of congressional power, or are to be regarded merely as caution signals—"admonitions"—which Congress need not always observe.[40] Madison's unsuccessful effort to add a counterpart of the First Amendment to the Constitution, his Proposal XIV prohibiting the states from infringing the rights of conscience, and freedom of speech and press, strikingly evidences his concern for their fullest protection. For him, the suppression of individuality was the deadly enemy of the spirit, making a mockery of the dignity of man. Hence his warning that, because a representative government like ours expresses the majority will, "The prescriptions in favor of liberty ought to be levelled against that quarter where the greatest danger lies, namely, that which possesses the highest prerogative of power. But this is not found in either the Executive or Legislative departments of Government, but in the body of the people, operating by the majority against the minority."[41]

Besides the First Amendment guarantees, only three specifics of the federal list, as such, have so far been held to be absorbed by the due process clause. Due process applies to the states the Fifth Amendment's requirement that "just compensation" shall be paid for private property taken for public use.[42] Thus the Fourteenth Amendment imposes the requirement which Marshall held in *Barron v. Baltimore* that the Federal Constitution did not originally impose upon the states. Due process requires the states to appoint counsel for an accused charged with an offense punishable by death, in accordance with the Sixth Amendment's requirement that an accused shall have "the assistance of counsel for his defense."[43] Finally, due process applies to the states the Fourth Amendment's guarantees against unreasonable searches and seizures. After holding in 1914 that the Fourth Amendment was not directed against state officials,[44] the Court in 1949 held that "The security of one's privacy against arbitrary intrusion by the police . . . is . . . implicit in 'the concept of ordered liberty' and as such enforceable against the States through the Due Process Clause."[45]

But considerations of federalism have thus far overborne the arguments in favor of the extension, as such, of the rest of the list. It may surprise many of you that some of these should not be regarded as among "the fundamental principles of liberty and justice which lie at the base of all our civil and political institutions."[46] For example, the right to trial by jury, highly valued by most of us, has been said not to be fundamental. The Court has held that the Seventh Amendment's requirement of a common law jury in civil causes does not apply to the states.[47] Many states try civil causes before juries of less than twelve and have abolished the common law requirement of a unanimous verdict. Perhaps Madison would have agreed that a proper deference to states' rights justified this holding as to the Seventh Amendment. One doubts, however, that he would be as readily reconciled to the Court's dicta that the Sixth Amendment's guarantee to one accused of crime of the right to trial by a jury of his peers is not binding on the states. These dicta say not only that the Fourteenth

79

Amendment does not absorb this guarantee, but indeed that the Constitution does not prevent a state from abolishing trial by jury in criminal causes altogether.[48] You will recall that Madison's rejected Proposal XIV embodied protections against state power not only for conscience, speech, and press, but also provided that "No State shall infringe the right of trial by Jury in criminal cases." The right of the accused to trial by jury was, said Madison, "as essential to secure the liberty of the people as any one of the pre-existent rights of nature."[49] The Court's extension to the states of the First Amendment's protections accords with Madison's judgment that indeed neither liberty nor justice would exist if these guarantees were sacrificed. It remains to be seen whether his judgment will also be confirmed if the Court is ever faced with a case in which a state has abolished trial by jury for serious criminal offenses.

The Court has held that the Sixth Amendment's guarantee of the right of an accused to have the assistance of court-appointed counsel for his defense is not, in non-capital cases, a fundamental principle absorbed by the Fourteenth Amendment.[50] It is only " 'where the gravity of the crime and other factors—such as the age and education of the defendant, the conduct of the court or the prosecuting officials, and the complicated nature of the offense charged and the possible defenses thereto—render criminal proceedings without counsel so apt to result in injustice as to be fundamentally unfair'. . . ." that the state has been held to have denied due process to a defendant tried for a noncapital offense.[51]

Only three weeks ago, I recorded my disagreement with this limitation of the extension of this specific of the Sixth Amendment to the states.[52] Rawle may have been in error in believing in 1825 that the Constitution without the Fourteenth Amendment imposed upon the states a duty to provide counsel in all state prosecutions. But none can deny Rawle's picture of the perilous position of the accused who must defend himself without a lawyer against the might of the state. "The most innocent man," Rawle said, "pressed by the awful solemnities of a public accusation and trial, may be incapable of supporting his own cause. He may be utterly unfit to cross-examine the witnesses against him, to point out the contradictions or defects of their testimony, and to counteract it by properly introducing and applying his own."[53] Without the help of a lawyer, all the other safeguards of a fair trial may be empty.

And it is not the due process clause that is alone involved here. The equal protection clause of the Fourteenth Amendment is also implicated. For a state cannot, consistently with the Federal Constitution, deny a citizen accused of crime the right to the assistance of counsel if he can afford to pay his own lawyer. The victims of the limitation upon the state's obligation to provide counsel are the indigent—they are the helpless, the weak, the outnumbered in our society.

The result of our decisions is to refuse a State the power to force a person into a criminal trial without a lawyer if he wants one and can afford to hire one, but to deny the same protection to an accused who is too poor to retain counsel. This draws a line between rich and poor that is repugnant to due process. The need of counsel is the same, whatever the economic status of the accused. If due process requires that a rich man who wants a lawyer be allowed the opportunity to obtain one before he is tried, why should not due process give the same protection to the accused who is indigent?[54]

A state may violate the equal protection clause if it fails at its expense to provide a convicted indigent defendant with a transcript of the trial proceedings for purposes of appeal.[55] The denial of counsel to an indigent accused seems almost to be an a fortiori case of the violation of the guarantee of equal protection of the laws.

The test of "fundamental unfairness" as a criterion applied to state prosecutions is not unique to cases involving the denial of counsel. For example, the values underlying the Fifth Amendment's privilege against self-incrimination are sufficiently absorbed by the due process clause to invalidate a state conviction obtained with the aid of a confession, however true, which was secured from the accused by duress or coercion. The Court has said, "The abhorrence of society to the use of involuntary confessions does not turn alone on their inherent untrustworthiness. It also turns on the deep-rooted feeling that the police must obey the law while enforcing the law; that in the end life and liberty can be as much endangered from illegal methods used to convict those thought to be criminals as from the actual criminals themselves."[56]

One may well ask why some of the safeguards for the just administration of criminal laws should be absorbed not at all, or only partially, in due process, when the protections of the First Amendment are absorbed in full. The Court has certainly recognized the paramount importance of procedural safeguards in criminal prosecutions. The Court has forged standards for federal prosecutions which go even beyond the demands of the Federal Bill of Rights as presently construed.[57] True, these standards have been fashioned under the Court's inherent powers to supervise the administration of justice in the lower federal courts, while intervention in the administration of the criminal laws of the states implicates considerations of federalism. But federalism should not be raised to the plane of an absolute, nor the Bill of Rights be reduced to a precatory trust, and the Court within the last half-century has dealt increasingly with state administration of criminal justice in constitutional terms.[58]

The history of the Court's treatment of the application of the Fourth Amendment to the states is a good example. I have mentioned that in 1914 the Court held that the "Fourth Amendment is not directed to individual misconduct of . . . [state] officials. Its limitations reach the Federal Government and its agencies."[59] But, in 1949, the Court held that the due process clause had asborbed the Fourth Amendment's protections.[60] The 1914 decision had also held that evidence illegally seized by state officers might be received in a federal prosecution. Last Term, the Court reconsidered this holding, now that the Fourth Amendment's protections are held to apply to the states, and held that evidence seized in violation of that amendment, whether by federal or state officers, is not to be received in a federal prosecution.[61]

However, the 1949 decision left the states free to use in state courts evidence illegally obtained by state officers, if permitted under the state's rules of evidence. In other words, the exclusionary rule has not thus far been held to be a constitutional requirement woven into the Fourth Amendment's guarantees. Last Term's decision excluding the evidence in a federal prosecution was expressly grounded in the Court's inherent authority to supervise the administration of justice in federal courts and not on the Constitution.

Should the exclusionary rule be treated as a mere rule of evidence or does it take on constitutional mien in the context of the Fourth Amendment? There are members of the Court who insist that the rule must be treated as a constitutional requisite or the 1949 extension of the Fourth Amendment's protections to state power has been a meaningless exercise.[62] They point out that state officers have little incentive to obey the Fourth Amendment's commands if evidence seized in defiance of them may be used against the victims in state courts. Those who find it surprising that a state should be allowed to send a man to prison or to his death on evidence which state officials have obtained in disregard of the Constitution of the United States believe that inevitably the Court must reconsider its 1949 holding.*

Fifty-four of the ninety-two Justices who have sat on the Court have participated in decisions which have considered the

* Justice Brennan's lecture was delivered on February 15, 1961. On June 19, 1961 the prophecy implied in this paragraph came true. Overruling its earlier holdings, the Supreme Court decided that a State conviction based on illegally obtained evidence was unconstitutional. Mapp v. Ohio, 367 U.S. 643 (1961).—Ed.

application to the states of one or more of the federal list. For all of these Justices, decision has involved choice among competing values. Some have claimed for due process that its special character, to use words Cardozo employed in another context, is "its power of adaptation, its suppleness, its play."[63] Federalism makes its own contribution to the preservation of our freedoms. The specifics of the Bill of Rights so far absorbed in due process have enhanced, not diminished, that contribution. The absorption of more can only further increase respect for our federalism. As Mr. Justice Schaefer of Illinois said in his Holmes Lecture at Harvard two years ago:

> Considerations of federalism of course remain important. But in the world today they must be measured against the competing demands arising out of the relation of the United States to the rest of the world. The quality of a nation's civilization can be largely measured by the methods it uses in the enforcement of its criminal law. That measurement is not taken merely in retrospect by social historians of the future. It is taken from day to day by the peoples of the world, and to them the criminal procedure sanctioned by any of our states is the procedure sanctioned by the United States.[64]

The Court has other compelling reasons for the application to the states of more of the specifics of the Bill of Rights. The absence in our country of the turbulence witnessed in other lands cannot obscure the fact that crises at hand and in prospect are creating, and will create, more and more collisions between the citizen and his government. The need for vigilance to prevent government from whittling away the rights of the individual was never greater. Today, as rarely before, case after case comes to the Court which finds the individual battling to vindicate a claim under the Bill of Rights against the powers of government, federal and state.

The Bill of Rights is the primary source of expressed information as to what is meant by constitutional liberty. The safeguards enshrined in it are deeply etched in the foundations of America's freedoms. Among the important specifics of the Bill of Rights still not fully applied to the states are those which are pertinent to the standards which should govern the administration of criminal justice. Each is a protection with centuries of history behind it, often dearly bought with the blood and lives of people determined to prevent oppression by their rulers. Would Madison have thought that the right of a person not to be twice put in jeopardy of life or limb for the same offense; not to be compelled in any criminal case to be a witness against one's self; as an accused, to enjoy the right in criminal prosecutions to a speedy and public trial by an impartial jury of twelve, to be informed of the nature and cause of the accusation, to be confronted with the witnesses against him, to have compulsory process for obtaining witnesses in his favor, and to have the assistance of counsel for his defense, were rights unnecessary to "the very essence of a scheme of ordered liberty," or that any was not among "the fundamental principles of liberty and justice which lie at the base of all our civil and political institutions," or not among those personal immunities which are "so rooted in the traditions and conscience of our people as to be ranked as fundamental"? In any event, what due process under the Fourteenth Amendment meant to the wisdom of other days cannot be its measure to the vision of our time. The importance of keeping aglow the fires of freedom was never greater. Excessive emphasis upon states' rights must not make the process of absorption "a license to the judiciary to administer a watered-down, subjective version of the individual guarantees of the Bill of Rights when state cases come before" the Court.[65]

It is reason for deep satisfaction that many of the states effectively enforce the counterparts in state constitutions of the specifics of the Bill of Rights. Indeed, some have been applied by states to an extent beyond that required of the national government by the corresponding federal guarantee.[66] But too many state practices fall far short. Far too many cases come from the states to the Supreme Court presenting dismal pictures of official lawlessness, of illegal searches and seizures, illegal detentions attended by prolonged interrogation and coerced admissions of guilt, of the denial of counsel, and downright brutality.[67] Judicial self-restraint which defers too much to the sovereign powers of the states and reserves judicial intervention for only the most revolting cases will not serve to enhance Madison's priceless gift of "the great rights of mankind secured under this Constitution."[68] For these secure the only climate in which the law of freedom can exist.

5

THE BILL OF RIGHTS AND THE MILITARY

Earl Warren

I T IS almost a commonplace to say that free government is on trial for its life. But it is the truth. And it has been so throughout history. What is almost as certain: It will probably be true throughout the foreseeable future. Why should this be so? Why is it that, over the centuries of world history, the right to liberty that our Declaration of Independence declares to be "inalienable" has been more often abridged than enforced?

One important reason, surely, is that the members of a free society are called upon to bear an extraordinarily heavy responsibility, for such a society is based upon the reciprocal self-imposed discipline of both the governed and their government. Many nations in the past have attempted to develop democratic institutions, only to lose them when either the people or their government lapsed from the rigorous self-control that is essential to the maintenance of a proper relation between freedom and order. Such failures have produced the totalitarianism or the anarchy that, however masked, are the twin mortal enemies of an ordered liberty.

Our forebears, well understanding this problem, sought to solve it in unique fashion by incorporating the concept of mutual restraint into our Nation's basic Charter. In the body of our Constitution, the Founding Fathers insured that the Government would have the power necessary to govern. Most of them felt that the self-discipline basic to a democratic government of delegated powers was implicit in that document in the light of our Anglo-Saxon heritage. But our people wanted explicit assurances. The Bill of Rights was the result.

This act of political creation was a remarkable beginning. It was only that, of course, for every generation of Americans must preserve its own freedoms. In so doing, we must turn time and again to the Bill of Rights, for it is that document that solemnly sets forth the political consensus that is our heritage. Nor should we confine ourselves to examining the diverse, complicated, and sometimes subordinate issues that arise in the day-to-day application of the Bill of Rights. It is perhaps more important that we seek to understand in its fullness the nature of the spirit of liberty that gave that document its birth.

Thus it is in keeping with the high purposes of this great University that its School of Law sponsor a series of lectures emphasizing the role of the Bill of Rights in contemporary American life. And it is particularly appropriate, after the splendid lectures of Mr. Justice Black[1] and Mr. Justice Brennan[2] on the relationship of the Bill of Rights to the Federal and State Governments, respectively, that you should delegate to someone the task of discussing the relationship of the Bill of Rights to the military establishment. This is a relationship that, perhaps more than any other, has rapidly assumed increasing importance because of changing domestic and world conditions. I am honored to undertake the assignment, not because I claim any expertise in the field, but because I want to cooperate with you in your contribution to the cause of preserving the spirit as well as the letter of the Bill of Rights.

Determining the proper role to be assigned to the military in a democratic society has been a troublesome problem for every nation that has aspired to a free political life. The military establishment is, of course, a necessary organ of government; but the reach of its power must be carefully limited lest the delicate balance between freedom and order be upset. The maintenance of the balance is made more difficult by the fact that while the military serves the vital function of preserving the existence of the nation, it is, at the same time, the one element of government that exercises a type of authority not easily assimilated in a free society.

The critical importance of achieving a proper accommodation is apparent when one considers the corrosive effect upon liberty of exaggerated military power. In the last analysis, it is the military —or at least a militant organization of power—that dominates life in totalitarian countries regardless of their nominal political arrangements. This is true, moreover, not only with respect to Iron

Curtain countries, but also with respect to many countries that have all of the formal trappings of constitutional democracy.

Not infrequently in the course of its history the Supreme Court has been called upon to decide issues that bear directly upon the relationship between action taken in the name of the military and the protected freedoms of the Bill of Rights. I would like to discuss here some of the principal factors that have shaped the Court's response. From a broad perspective, it may be said that the questions raised in these cases are all variants of the same fundamental problem: Whether the disputed exercise of power is compatible with preservation of the freedoms intended to be insulated by the Bill of Rights.

I believe it is reasonably clear that the Court, in cases involving a substantial claim that protected freedoms have been infringed in the name of military requirements, has consistently recognized the relevance of a basic group of principles. For one, of course, the Court has adhered to its mandate to safeguard freedom from excessive encroachment by governmental authority. In these cases, the Court's approach is reinforced by the American tradition of the separation of the military establishment from, and its subordination to, civil authority. On the other hand, the action in question is generally defended in the name of military necessity, or, to put it another way, in the name of national survival. I suggest that it is possible to discern in the Court's decisions a reasonably consistent pattern for the resolution of these competing claims, and more, that this pattern furnishes a sound guide for the future. Moreover, these decisions reveal, I believe, that while the judiciary plays an important role in this area, it is subject to certain significant limitations, with the result that other organs of government and the people themselves must bear a most heavy responsibility.

Before turning to some of the keystone decisions of the Court, I think it desirable to consider for a moment the principle of separation and subordination of the military establishment, for it is this principle that contributes in a vital way to a resolution of the problems engendered by the existence of a military establishment in a free society.

It is significant that in our own hemisphere only our neighbor, Canada, and we ourselves have avoided rule by the military throughout our national existences. This is not merely happenstance. A tradition has been bred into us that the perpetuation of free government depends upon the continued supremacy of the civilian representatives of the people. To maintain this supremacy has always been a preoccupation of all three branches of our government. To strangers this might seem odd, since our country was born in war. It was the military that, under almost unbearable conditions, carried the burden of the Revolution and made possible our existence as a Nation.

But the people of the colonies had long been subjected to the intemperance of military power. Among the grievous wrongs of which they complained in the Declaration of Independence were that the King had subordinated the civil power to the military, that he had quartered troops among them in times of peace, and that through his mercenaries he had committed other cruelties. Our War of the Revolution was, in good measure, fought as a protest against standing armies. Moreover, it was fought largely with a civilian army, the militia, and its great Commander-in-Chief was a civilian at heart. After the War, he resigned his commission and returned to civilian life. In an emotion-filled appearance before the Congress, his resignation was accepted by its President, Thomas Mifflin, who, in a brief speech, emphasized Washington's qualities of leadership and, above all, his abiding respect for civil authority.[3] This trait was probably best epitomized when, just prior to the War's end, some of his officers urged Washington to establish a monarchy, with himself at its head. He not only turned a deaf ear to their blandishments, but his reply, called by historian Edward Channing "possibly, the grandest single thing in his whole career,"[4] stated that nothing had given him more painful sensations than the information that such notions existed in the army, and that he thought their proposal "big with the greatest mischiefs that can befall my Country."[5]

Such thoughts were uppermost in the minds of the Founding Fathers when they drafted the Constitution. Distrust of a standing army was expressed by many. Recognition of the danger from Indians and foreign nations caused them to authorize a national armed force begrudgingly. Their viewpoint is well summarized in the language of James Madison, whose name we honor in these lectures:

The veteran legions of Rome were an overmatch for the undisciplined valor of all other nations, and rendered her the mistress of the world. Not the less true is it, that the liberties of Rome proved the final victim of her military triumphs; and that the liberties of Europe, as far as they ever existed, have, with few exceptions, been the price of her military establishments. A standing force, therefore, is a dangerous, at the same time that it may be a necessary, provision. On the smallest scale it has its inconveniences. On an extensive scale its consequences may be fatal. On any scale it is an object of laudable circumspection and precaution. A wise nation will combine all these considerations; and, whilst it does not rashly preclude itself from any resource which may become essential to its safety, will exert all its prudence in diminishing both the necessity and the danger of resorting to one which may be inauspicious to its liberties.[6]

Their apprehensions found expression in the diffusion of the war powers granted the Government by the Constitution. The President was made the Commander-in-Chief of the armed forces. But Congress was given the power to provide for the common defense, to declare war, to make rules for the government and regulation of the land and naval forces, and to raise and support armies, with the added precaution that no appropriation could be made for the latter purpose for longer than two years at a time—as an antidote to a standing army. Further, provision was made for organizing and calling forth the state militia to execute the laws of the Nation in times of emergency.

93

Despite these safeguards, the people were still troubled by the recollection of the conditions that prompted the charge of the Declaration of Independence that the King had "effected to render the military independent and superior to the civil power." They were reluctant to ratify the Constitution without further assurances, and thus we find in the Bill of Rights Amendments II and III, specifically authorizing a decentralized militia, guaranteeing the right of the people to keep and bear arms, and prohibiting the quartering of troops in any house in time of peace without the consent of the owner. Other Amendments guarantee the right of the people to assemble, to be secure in their homes against unreasonable searches and seizures, and in criminal cases to be accorded a speedy and public trial by an impartial jury after indictment in the district and state wherein the crime was committed. The only exceptions made to these civilian trial procedures are for cases arising in the land and naval forces. Although there is undoubtedly room for argument based on the frequently conflicting sources of history, it is not unreasonable to believe that our Founders' determination to guarantee the preeminence of civil over military power was an important element that prompted adoption of the Constitutional Amendments we call the Bill of Rights.[7]

Civil supremacy has consistently been the goal of our Government from colonial days to these. As late as 1947, when the Department of Defense was established, Congress specifically provided for a civilian chief officer. And when President Truman asked the Congress for an amendment to make an exception for a soldier and statesman as great as the late George C. Marshall, serious debate followed before the Act was modified to enable him to become Secretary of Defense, and then only by a small majority of the total membership of the House and less than half of the Senate.[8] Those who opposed the amendment often expressed their high regard for General Marshall, but made known their fears concerning any deviation, even though temporary, from our traditional subordination of military to civil power.[9]

The history of our country does not indicate that there has ever been a widespread desire to change the relationship between the civil government and the military; and it can be fairly said that, with minor exceptions, military men throughout our history have not only recognized and accepted this relationship in the spirit of the Constitution, but that they have also cheerfully co-operated in preserving it.

Thus it is plain that the axiom of subordination of the military to the civil is not an anachronism. Rather, it is so deeply rooted in our national experience that it must be regarded as an essential constituent of the fabric of our political life.

But sometimes competing with this principle—and with the "Thou Shalt Nots" of the Bill of Rights—is the claim of military necessity. Where such a conflict is asserted before the Court, the basic problem has been, as I have indicated, to determine whether and how these competing claims may be resolved in the framework of a lawsuit.

Cases of this nature appear to me to be divisible into three broad categories. The first involves questions concerning the military establishment's treatment of persons who are concededly subject to military authority—what may be termed the vertical reach of the Bill of Rights within the military. These questions have been dealt with quite differently than the second category of disputes, involving what may be called the horizontal reach of the Bill of Rights. Cases of this type pose principally the question whether the complaining party is a proper subject of military authority. Finally, there are cases which do not, strictly speaking, involve the action of the military, but rather the action of other government agencies taken in the name of military necessity.

So far as the relationship of the military to its own personnel is concerned, the basic attitude of the Court has been that the latter's jurisdiction is most limited. Thus, the Supreme Court has adhered consistently to the 1863 holding of *Ex parte Vallandigham*[10] that it lacks jurisdiction to review by certiorari the decisions of military courts. The cases in which the Court has ordered the release of persons convicted by courts martial have, to date, been limited to instances in which it found lack of military jurisdiction over the person so tried, using the term "jurisdiction" in its narrowest sense. That is, they were all cases in which the defendant was found to be such that he was not constitutionally, or statutorily, amenable to military justice. Such was the classic formulation of the relation between civil courts and courts martial as expressed in *Dynes v. Hoover*,[11] decided in 1857.

This "hands off" attitude has strong historical support, of course. While I cannot here explore the matter completely, there is also no necessity to do so, since it is indisputable that the tradition of our country, from the time of the Revolution until now, has supported the military establishment's broad power to deal with its own personnel. The most obvious reason is that courts are ill-equipped to determine the impact upon discipline that any particular intrusion upon military authority might have. Many of the problems of the military society are, in a sense, alien to the problems with which the judiciary is trained to deal.

However, the obvious reason is not always the most important one. I suppose it cannot be said that the courts of today are more knowledgeable about the requirements of military discipline than the courts in the early days of the Republic. Nevertheless, events quite unrelated to the expertise of the judiciary have required a modification in the traditional theory of the autonomy of military authority.

These events can be expressed very simply in numerical terms. A few months after Washington's first inauguration, our army numbered a mere 672 of the 840 authorized by Congress.[12] Today, in dramatic contrast, the situation is this: Our armed forces number two and a half million;[13] every resident male is a potential member of the peacetime armed forces; such service may occupy a minimum of four per cent of the adult life of the average American male reaching draft age; reserve obligations extend over ten per cent of such a person's life;[14] and veterans are numbered in excess of twenty-two and a half million.[15] When the authority of the military has such a sweeping capacity for affecting the lives of our citizenry, the wisdom of treating the military establishment as an enclave beyond the reach of the civilian courts almost inevitably is drawn into question.

Thus it was hardly surprising to find that, in 1953, the Supreme Court indicated in *Burns v. Wilson*[16] that court martial proceedings could be challenged through habeas corpus actions brought in civil courts, if those proceedings had denied the defendant fundamental rights. The various opinions of the members of the Court in *Burns* are not, perhaps, as clear on this point as they might be. Nevertheless, I believe they do constitute recognition of the proposition that our citizens in uniform may not be stripped of basic rights simply because they have doffed their civilian clothes.

Despite *Burns*, however, it could hardly be expected that the regular federal judiciary would play a large role in regulating the military's treatment of its own personnel. The considerations militating against such intervention remain strong. Consequently, more important than *Burns* from a practical point of view was the action in 1951 of another guardian of the Bill of Rights, Congress, in enacting the Uniform Code of Military Justice and in establishing the Court of Military Appeals as a sort of civilian "Supreme Court" of the military.[17] The Code represents a diligent effort by Congress to insure that military justice is administered in accord with the demands of due process. Attesting to its success is the fact that since 1951 the number of habeas corpus petitions alleging a lack of fairness in courts martial has been quite insubstantial.[18] Moreover, I know of no case since the adoption of the Code in which a civil court has issued the writ on the basis of such a claim. This development is undoubtedly due in good part to the supervision of military justice by the Court of Military Appeals. Chief Judge Quinn of that Court has recently stated:

[M]ilitary due process begins with the basic rights and privileges defined in the federal constitution. It does not stop there. The letter and the background of the Uniform Code add their weighty demands to the requirements of a fair trial. Military due process is, thus, not synonymous with federal civilian due process. It is basically that, but something more, and something different.[19]

And the Court of Military Appeals has, itself, said unequivocally that "the protections in the Bill of Rights, except those which are expressly or by necessary implication inapplicable, are available to members of our armed forces."[20]

Thus our recent experience has shown, I believe, that the Court of Military Appeals can be an effective guarantor of our citizens' rights to due process when they are subjected to trial by court martial. Moreover, the establishment of a special court to review these cases obviates, at least to some extent, the objection of lack of familiarity by the reviewing tribunal with the special problems of the military. In this connection, I think it significant that, despite the expanded application of our civilian concepts of fair play to military justice, the Chairman of the Joint Chiefs of Staff, General Lemnitzer, declared not long ago:

I believe the Army and the American people can take pride in the positive strides that have been made in the application of military law under the Uniform Code of Military Justice. The Army today has achieved the highest state of discipline and good order in its history.[21]

These developments support my conviction that the guarantees of our Bill of Rights need not be considered antithetical to the maintenance of our defenses.

Nevertheless, we cannot fail to recognize how our burgeoning army has posed difficult and unique problems for the Court in the application of constitutional principles. Thus, you may recall the case of Specialist Girard,[22] who, having been sent to Japan by the

Army, contended that the Constitution entitled him to a trial by an American court martial for an offense committed on an American army reservation in Japan against a Japanese national. The surrender of Girard to Japanese authorities was consonant with well-established rules of international law, and the Court's opinion cited, as its authority, the decision of Chief Justice Marshall in *The Schooner Exchange*,[23] written in 1812. But the case brought to light some problems we should consider in the light of developments unforeseen at the time the Constitution was written: the world-wide deployment of our citizens, called to duty and sent to foreign lands for extended tours of service, who may, by administrative decision of American authorities, be delivered to foreign governments for trial.[24] We are fortunate that our experience in this area has generally been a happy one,[25] and thus, to date, these constitutional problems have been largely submerged.

However, unique constitutional questions are, at times, presented for decision, which questions are, in part, an outgrowth of our expanded military forces. One of the most recent of these arose in *Trop v. Dulles*,[26] decided in 1958. In that case the Court considered a provision of our law that acted automatically to denationalize a citizen convicted of wartime desertion by a court martial. Under this provision, over 7,000 men who had served in the Army alone, in World War II, were rendered stateless. It was the decision of the Court that, by this Act, Congress had exceeded its constitutional powers by depriving citizens of their birthright. Four members of the Court, of which I was one, expressed the view that this law, effectively denying the person's rights to have rights, was a cruel and unusual punishment proscribed by the Eighth Amendment. The need for military discipline was considered an inadequate foundation for expatriation.

The *Trop* case was an example, really, of how the Court has generally dealt with problems apart from the authority of the military in dealing with "its own." Rather, it was in the line of decisions dealing with attempts of our civilian Government to extend military authority into other areas. In these cases we find factors different from those the Court must consider persuasive in review of a soldier's disciplinary conviction by court martial. The contending parties still advance the same general argument: protected liberties versus military necessity. Here, however, the tradition of exclusive authority of the military over its uniformed personnel is generally not directly relevant. Here, the Court has usually been of the view that it can and should make its own judgment, at least to some degree, concerning the weight a claim of military necessity is to be given.

The landmark decision in this field was, of course, *Ex parte Milligan*,[27] decided in 1866. It established firmly the principle that when civil courts are open and operating, resort to military tribunals for the prosecution of civilians is impermissible. The events giving rise to the *Milligan* case occurred while we were in the throes of a great war. However, the military activities of that war had been confined to a certain section of the country; in the remainder, the civil government operated normally. In passing upon the validity of a military conviction returned against Milligan outside the theater of actual combat, the Court recognized that no "graver question" was ever previously before it. And yet the Court, speaking through Mr. Justice Davis, reminded us that

by the protection of the law human rights are secured; withdraw that protection, and they are at the mercy of wicked rulers, or the clamor of an excited people. If there was law to justify . . . [Milligan's] military trial, it is not our province to interfere; if there was not, it is our duty to declare the nullity of their whole proceedings.[28]

I do not propose to discuss in detail other cases that have been decided in a wartime context, for the risk is too great that they lie outside the mainstream of American judicial thought. War is, of course, a pathological condition for our Nation. Military judgments sometimes breed action that, in more stable times, would be regarded as abhorrent. Judges cannot detach themselves from such judgments, although by hindsight, from the vantage point of more tranquil times, they might conclude that some actions advanced in the name of national survival had in fact overridden the strictures of due process.[29]

Obviously such a charge could not be made against the Court in the *Milligan* case. However, some have pointed to cases like the companion decisions of *Hirabayashi v. United States*[30] and *Korematsu v. United States*[31] as aberrational. There, you will recall, the Court sustained the program under which, shortly after the attack on Pearl Harbor, over 100,000 Japanese nationals and citizens of that ancestry living in the western United States were, under Executive Order, with congressional sanction, placed under curfew and later excluded from areas within 750 miles of the Pacific Coast or confined in government detention camps.

Whatever may be the correct view of the specific holding of those cases, their importance for present purposes lies in a more general consideration. These decisions demonstrate dramatically that there are some circumstances in which the Court will, in effect, conclude that it is simply not in a position to reject descriptions by the Executive of the degree of military necessity. Thus, in a case like *Hirabayashi*, only the Executive is qualified to determine whether, for example, an invasion is imminent. In such a situation, where time is of the essence, if the Court is to deny the asserted right of the military authorities, it must be on the theory that the claimed justification, though factually unassailable, is insufficient. Doubtless cases might arise in which such a response would be the only permissible one. After all, the truism that the end does not justify the means has at least as respectable a lineage as the dictum that the power to wage war is the power to wage war successfully.[32] But such cases would be extraordinary indeed.

The consequence of the limitations under which the Court must sometimes operate in this area is that other agencies of government must bear the primary responsibility for determining whether specific actions they are taking are consonant with our Constitution. To put it another way, the fact that the Court rules in a case like *Hirabayashi* that a given program is constitutional, does not necessarily answer the question whether, in a broader sense, it actually is.

There is still another lesson to be learned from cases like *Hirabayashi*. Where the circumstances are such that the Court must accept uncritically the Government's description of the magnitude of the military need, actions may be permitted that restrict individual liberty in a grievous manner. Consequently, if judicial review is to constitute a meaningful restraint upon unwarranted encroachments upon freedom in the name of military necessity, situations in which the judiciary refrains from examining the merit of the claim of necessity must be kept to an absolute minimum. In this connection, it is instructive to compare the result in *Hirabayashi* with the result in cases that have been decided outside the context of war.

In times of peace, the factors leading to an extraordinary deference to claims of military necessity have naturally not been as weighty. This has been true even in the all too imperfect peace that has been our lot for the past fifteen years—and quite rightly so, in my judgment. It is instructive to recall that our Nation at the time of the Constitutional Convention was also faced with formidable problems. The English, the French, the Spanish, and various tribes of hostile Indians were all ready and eager to subvert or occupy the fledgling Republic. Nevertheless, in that environment, our Founding Fathers conceived a Constitution and Bill of Rights replete with provisions indicating their determination to protect human rights. There was no call for a garrison state in those times of precarious peace. We should heed no such call now. If we were to fail in these days to enforce the freedom that until now has been the American citizen's birthright, we should be abandoning for the foreseeable future the constitutional balance of powers and rights in whose name we arm.

Moreover, most of the cases the Court has decided during this period indicate that such a capitulation to the claim of military necessity would be a needless sacrifice. These cases have not been argued or decided in an emergency context comparable to the early 1940's. There has been time, and time provides a margin of safety. There has been time for the Government to be put to the proof with respect to its claim of necessity; there has been time for reflection; there has been time for the Government to adjust to any adverse decision. The consequence is that the claim of necessity has generally not been put to the Court in the stark terms of a *Hirabayashi* case.[33]

An excellent example of the approach adopted by the Court in the recent years of peacetime tension is its disposition of the various cases raising the question of court-martial jurisdiction over civilian dependents and employees of the armed forces overseas. Such jurisdiction was explicitly granted by the Uniform Code of Military Justice, and hence the issue was whether the statutory provision was constitutional.

In what the Court came to recognize as a hasty decision, this exercise of jurisdiction was at first sustained in the most striking of the cases presenting the problem—the trial of the wife of an American soldier for a capital offense. During the summer following that decision, a rehearing was considered and finally ordered. The next June, the rewritten, landmark decision of *Reid v. Covert*[34] struck down this exercise of military jurisdiction as an unconstitutional expansion of Congress' power to provide for the government of the armed forces. In 1960, *Reid v. Covert* was followed by the Court in similarly invalidating court-martial convictions of civilians accompanying and those employed by our services overseas, whether or not the offenses for which they had been convicted were punishable by death.[35]

Several features of these cases are worthy of note. First of all, the urgency of wartime was absent. Extended analysis and deliberation on the part of the parties and the Court were possible. Secondly, while, of course, the Government rested heavily upon a claim of military necessity, that claim could not be pressed with the same force that it was in *Hirabayashi*. Alternative methods of dealing with the military's problems could be considered. Indeed, the Court itself suggested a possible alternative in one of its opinions—the creation of a military service akin to the Seabees to secure the services theretofore performed by civilians. And finally, the extension of military jurisdiction for which the Government contended was extraordinarily broad. At that time, there were 450,000 dependents and 25,000 civilian employees overseas.[36] We could not safely deal with such a problem on the basis of what General Anthony Wayne did or did not do to camp followers at frontier forts in the last decade of the 18th century. In short, as in the case of trials of persons who are concededly part of the military, the burgeoning of our military establishment produced a situation so radically different from what the country had known in its distant past that the Court was required to return to first principles in coming to its judgment.

Another decision of the Court that is of significance in connection with the considerations I have been discussing was *Toth v. Quarles*.[37] There the Court held that a veteran holding an honorable discharge could not be recalled to active duty for the sole purpose of subjecting him to a court martial prosecution for offenses committed prior to his discharge. The question was of enormous significance in the context of present day circumstances, for the ranks of our veterans are estimated to number more than twenty-two-and-a-half-million. Thus a decision adverse to the petitioner would have left millions of former servicemen helpless before some latter-day revival of old military charges. So far as the claim of military necessity was concerned, the facts were such that the Court regarded itself as competent to deal with the problem directly. Mr. Justice Black, speaking for the Court, said:

It is impossible to think that the discipline of the Army is going to be disrupted, its morale impaired, or its orderly processes disturbed, by giving ex-servicemen the benefits of a civilian court trial when they are actually civilians . . . Free countries of the world have tried to restrict military tribunals to the narrowest jurisdiction deemed absolutely essential to maintaining discipline among troops in active service.[38]

Attempts at extension of military control have not, of course, been confined to the field of criminal justice, nor have all of them been decided on constitutional grounds. *Harmon v. Brucker*[39] brought to the court the Army's claim that it had the authority to issue to a draftee a discharge less than honorable on the basis of certain activities in which the soldier was said to have engaged prior to his induction, and which the Army thought made him a security risk. Again, the gravity of the constitutional issues raised was underscored by the existence of our system of peacetime conscription, for the sustaining of the Army's claim would have affirmed its authority to affect the pre-service political activities of every young American. A notable feature of the case was that the Solicitor General conceded that, if the Court had jurisdiction to rule upon the action of the Secretary of the Army, his action should be held to be unconstitutional. Thus the Government's case was placed entirely upon the asserted necessity for, and tradition of, the exclusive authority of the Secretary to act with unreviewable discretion in cases of this nature. The Court, however, found it unnecessary to reach constitutional issues. It disposed of the case on the non-constitutional ground that the Secretary lacked statutory authority to condition the type of discharge he issued upon any behavior other than that in which the soldier engaged during his period of service. Such emphasis upon proper directives by Congress with respect to these problems, may be regarded as, in part, a further reflection of the principle of subordination of the military establishment to civil authority.

I cannot, of course, discuss more than a handful of the Supreme

Court decisions bearing upon the military establishment's efforts to extend the scope of its authority in one way or another beyond service members. The cases I have dealt with, however, disclose what I regard as the basic elements of the approach the Court has followed with reasonable consistency. There are many other decisions that echo that approach, and there are some, to be sure, that seem inconsistent with it. But I would point to *Duncan v. Kahanamoku*,[40] in which the Court held, in the spirit of *Milligan*, although on non-constitutional grounds, that, after the Pearl Harbor attack, civilians in the Hawaiian Islands were subject to trial only in civilian courts, once those courts were open. And, of course, there have been a number of cases that, like *Harmon v. Brucker*, emphasize the Court's view that the military, like any other organ of government, must adhere strictly to its legislative mandate.[41]

On the whole, it seems to me plain that the Court has viewed the separation and subordination of the military establishment as a compelling principle. When this principle supports an assertion of substantial violation of a precept of the Bill of Rights, a most extraordinary showing of military necessity in defense of the Nation has been required for the Court to conclude that the challenged action in fact squared with the injunctions of the Constitution. While situations may arise in which deference by the Court is compelling, the cases in which this has occurred demonstrate that such a restriction upon the scope of review is pregnant with danger to individual freedom. Fortunately, the Court has generally been in a position to apply an exacting standard. Thus, although the dangers inherent in the existence of a huge military establishment may well continue to grow, we need have no feeling of hopelessness. Our tradition of liberty has remained strong through recurring crises. We need only remain true to it.

The last phase of the problem of the military in our society—the relationship of the military to civil government and affairs—

is much more complex, and also perhaps much more important, than the subjects I have just discussed.

This relationship of the military to the rest of us raises issues that are less graphic, less tangible, less amenable to review or control by the courts. This aspect of the problem encompasses not only actions taken by our civil government in the name of defense that may impinge upon individual rights, but also matters such as the influence exerted on the civil government by uniformed personnel and the suppliers of arms. Such problems are not always clearly visible. Nor is the impact of our enormous financial, human and resource commitment to the needs of defense easy to measure.[42] Moreover, these problems often do not arise in a factual context suitable for a lawsuit and judicial review. Still, "cases and controversies" have occasionally arisen in recent years that suggest the magnitude of the difficulties we face.

Looking first at perhaps the broadest aspect of the problems generated by our defense needs, we could consider the question whether the industries basic to our defense are in all respects to be treated as "private" industry. In wartime, the total mobilization of our economy with its rationing, allocation of materials and manpower, and price and wage controls are acceptable restrictions for a free society locked in combat. The just compensation and due process provisions of the Constitution may be strained at such times. Are they to receive similar diminished deference in these days of "cold war"? This alone is a subject worthy of the most extended discussion. I can do no more here than suggest its pertinency. But it has been thrust upon the Court with a requirement for prompt decision in recent years.

You will recall the case of *Youngstown Sheet & Tube v. Sawyer*,[43] in which, in the midst of our military operations in Korea, the Court held that the President lacked the power, without specific Congressional sanction, to seize and operate the Nation's steel industry following its shut-down by a nation-wide strike. The numerous and lengthy opinions of the various members of the

Court reveal the tremendous complexity of the issues such a case presents. And on what may the courts rely in such litigation? Consider these words from Mr. Justice Jackson's concurring opinion:

A judge . . . may be surprised at the poverty of really useful and unambiguous authority applicable to concrete problems . . . as they actually present themselves. Just what our forefathers did envision, or would have envisioned had they foreseen modern conditions, must be divined from materials almost as enigmatic as the dreams Joseph was called upon to interpret for Pharoah. A century and a half of partisan debate and scholarly speculation yields no net result but only supplies more or less apt quotations from respected sources on each side of any question. They largely cancel each other. And court decisions are indecisive because of the judicial practice of dealing with the largest questions in the most narrow way.[44]

The result in the *Youngstown* case may be compared to the decision seven years later in *United Steelworkers of America v. United States*,[45] a decision reached during a time that no actual armed conflict engaged this country. There, the Court upheld a finding that since one per cent of the Nation's steel industry output was needed for defense purposes, the President had the authority, under the Taft-Hartley Act, to enjoin the union from continuing its strike, at least for eighty days. The critical factor upon which the injunction was based and sustained was a determination that even the temporary unavailability of one per cent of the industry's output might imperil the Nation's safety. Considerations that the injunction might infringe upon the workers' constitutional rights of free association, or perhaps the right *not* to work, fell, at least temporarily, before these findings. Should Congressional intervention—the difference between the *Youngstown* and *Steelworkers* cases—be so decisive? Would recourse to Taft-Hartley or other legislation by President Truman in 1952 have avoided the issues that made the *Youngstown* case so difficult? We need not, indeed cannot, answer that now. However, these cases illustrate the extent to which public and private interests merge and clash in controversies so vitally affecting the security of the Nation. The resolution of such cases is made no more simple or certain by the multitude of considerations that, while indisputably relevant, are outside the records before the courts.

On a less grand scale than the steel industry litigation, but perhaps no less significant, are the cases that have stemmed from the competition between the claims of national security and personal rights. The bulk of the many recent decisions concerning the contempt power of Congressional committees provides a graphic illustration. Some believe that these cases may be disposed of by the Court's balancing of the security of the Nation against the freedom of the individual litigant. If these are the appropriate weights to put in the scales, it is not surprising that the balance is usually struck against the individual. If balance we must, I wonder whether on the individual's side we might not also place the importance of our survival as a free nation. The issue, as I see it, is not the individual against society; it is rather the wise accommodation of the necessities of physical survival with the requirements of spiritual survival. Lincoln once asked, "[Is] it possible to lose the nation and yet preserve the Constitution?"[46] His rhetorical question called for a negative answer no less than its corollary: "Is it possible to lose the Constitution and yet preserve the Nation?" Our Constitution and Nation are one. Neither can exist without the other. It is with this thought in mind that we should gauge the claims of those who assert that national security requires what our Constitution appears to condemn.

Naturally the radiations of security requirements have come before the Court in contexts other than Congressional investigations. Even more closely connected with the defense effort have been the decisions concerning the right to employment in government and industry.

One may compare, for example, the 1959 case of *Greene v.*

McElroy[47] with last Term's decision in *Cafeteria Workers v. Mc-Elroy*.[48] In the former, a serious constitutional issue was raised by the Navy's action in denying, on questionable grounds, security clearance to a privately employed aeronautical engineer. This, in turn, effectively precluded him from pursuing his occupation. The Court was able, however, to dispose of the case on the non-constitutional ground that requirements of confrontation prescribed by existing law had wrongfully been ignored.[49] In *Cafeteria Workers*, on the other hand, where a short-order cook employed by a concessionaire on a military base was summarily refused further security clearance without hearing, explanation, or opportunity to rebut, the Court reached the constitutional question and, by a five-to-four vote, decided it against the employee. I joined Mr. Justice Brennan's dissent, which took the position that the Court, while conceding petitioner's right not to be injured arbitrarily by the Government, in fact made that right non-enforceable by refusing to accord petitioner any procedural protection.

One of the principal difficulties presented by these "security risk" cases is that the claim of necessity takes the form of an assertion of the right of secrecy. Thus, the claim, by its very nature, tends to restrict the ability of the Court to evaluate its merit. This in turns impairs the efficacy of judicial review as an instrument for preserving the guarantees of the Bill of Rights. While the dilemma is in some cases serious, *Cafeteria Workers*, the most recent expression of the Court's views on the subject, does not, in my judgment, represent a satisfactory guidepost for resolution of the problem.

Our enormous national commitment of defense will, of course, pose still additional, difficult problems for the courts. We have, in the past considered,[50] and will probably be called upon in the future to review, cases arising out of the effort to accord our large number of veterans special compensation or preferences in return for their service to the country. While recognizing the need for such programs, we are also asked to consider to what extent such preferences impinge on opportunities of other citizens, whose public service and welfare are no less deserving of recognition. Questions concerning the review of military procurement, in the light of claims of emergency need, expert judgment and secrecy of information are still largely unresolved. The problem of the extent to which members of the armed forces may properly express their political views to other troops, particularly subordinates in the chain of command, and to the public at large, are subjects of controversy. Questions of the right of the people to know what their government is doing, their right to travel, speak, congregate, believe, and dissent will arise again and again. It is to the courts that the task of adjudicating many of these rights is delegated. I am one who believes firmly that the Court must be vigilant against neglect of the requirements of our Bill of Rights and the personal rights that document was intended to guarantee for all time. Legislative or executive action eroding our citizens' rights in the name of security cannot be placed on a scale that weighs the public's interest against that of the individual in a sort of "count the heads" fashion. Democracy under our Constitution calls for judicial deference to the coordinate branches of the Government and their judgment of what is essential to the protection of the Nation. But it calls no less for a steadfast protection of those fundamentals imbedded in the Constitution, so incorporated for the express purpose of insulating them from possible excesses of the moment. Our history has demonstrated that we must be as much on guard against the diminution of our rights through excessive fears for our security and a reliance on military solutions for our problems by the civil government, as we are against the usurpation of civil authority by the army. That is the important lesson of the Court cases, most of which have arisen not through the initiative of the military seeking power for itself, but rather through governmental authorization for intervention of military considerations in affairs properly reserved to our civilian institutions.

In concluding, I must say that I have, of course, not touched upon every type of situation having some relation to our military establishment which the Court considers. Those to which I have pointed might suggest to some that the Court has at times exceeded its role in this area. My view of the matter is the opposite. I see how limited is the role that the courts can truly play in protecting the heritage of our people against military supremacy. In our democracy it is still the Legislature and the elected Executive who have the primary responsibility for fashioning and executing policy consistent with the Constitution. Only an occasional aberration from norms of operation is brought before the Court by some zealous litigant. Thus we are sometimes provided with opportunities for reiterating the fundamental principles on which our country was founded and has grown mighty. But the day-to-day job of upholding the Constitution really lies elsewhere. It rests, realistically, on the shoulders of every citizen.

President Eisenhower, as he left the White House only a year ago, urged the American people to be alert to the changes that come about by reason of the coalescence of military and industrial power. His words were these:

[T]his conjunction of an immense military establishment and a large arms industry is new in the American experience. The total influence —economic, political, even spiritual—is felt in every city, every state house, every office of the Federal Government. . . . [W]e must not fail to comprehend . . . [the] grave implications. Our toil, resources and livelihood are all involved; so is the very structure of our society.

[W]e must guard against the acquisition of unwarranted influence . . . by the military-industrial complex. . . .

We must never let the weight of this combination endanger our liberties or democratic processes. We should take nothing for granted. Only an alert and knowledgeable citizenry can compel the proper meshing of the . . . machinery of defense with our peaceful methods and goals, so that security and liberty may prosper together.[51]

Coming from one who was our great Field Commander in World War II and for eight years Commander-in-Chief as President of the United States, these words should find lodgment in the mind of every American. It is also significant that both his predecessor and his successor have conveyed the same thought in slightly different words.[52] I am sure that none of them thought for a moment that anyone was deliberately trying to change the relationship between the military and the civil government. But they realized, as we all must, that our freedoms must be protected not only against deliberate destruction but also against unwitting erosion.

We may happily note that the Constitution has remarkably weathered a variety of crises. Some were as acute as those we face today. Today, as always, the people, no less than their courts, must remain vigilant to preserve the principles of our Bill of Rights, lest in our desire to be secure we lose our ability to be free.

6

THE BILL OF RIGHTS IS NOT ENOUGH

William O. Douglas

I. PEOPLE long submerged, who finally win their independence, seem at times to lose their moorings. Under colonial rule they work for independence as if possessed. Yet once the bonds are cast down, there is often bewilderment. What is this new thing called freedom? The suspicions once directed against colonial rulers become doubts about one's neighbors. Some soon realize that equality, not freedom alone, was all along the real goal. Yet even after independence, equality seems a fragile thing without institutions to espouse and defend it.

The majority, though freed of colonial domination or control, becomes an ominous force to behold, when it holds sovereignty in its hands and exercises it without restraint. As deTocqueville wrote:

> A majority taken collectively is only an individual, whose opinions, and frequently whose interests, are opposed to those of another individual, who is styled a minority.[1]

Preventive detention (written into some of the new constitutions and held constitutional by the Supreme Court of Ghana in 1961) is as severe whatever the race or nationality of the committing magistrate. The bill of attainder, by which Nkrumah in 1957 banished two of his political opponents, was as convenient to the new leader as it was to a Stuart King and as harsh on an African as on an Englishman or American. The so-called "precautionary" arrests made by Ayub when unrest reached East Pakistan in 1962 landed people in jails as uncomfortable as any the British had maintained. Ex post facto laws are no monopoly of the Communist regimes which apply them relentlessly. The military *junta* that seized control of South Korea in 1960 passed a series of ex post facto laws and constituted the Special Court (later renamed the Revolutionary Court) to apply them.

Each nation apparently must learn for itself the familiar lesson:

> If men are to remain civilized, or to become so, the art of associating together must grow and improve in the same ratio in which the equality of conditions is increased.[2]

Disorder is the aftermath of revolution whether power is forcibly or peacefully transferred. An elite—an educated class with knowledge of government—can provide leadership. Controls or checks and balances can be written into the charter, so as to curb legislative, executive, and judicial power. Yet they have force and meaning only if the *consensus* that brought them into being is a *consensus* that suffers them to be the way of life. Even that *consensus* may not be enough. Pakistan, with both a promising Constitution and a distinguished elite that was legally trained, became overnight a dictatorship when Ayub tore up the Constitution and a Bill of Rights and took unto himself all executive, legislative, and judicial power. The same happened in Burma in 1962 (for the second time) when Ne Win ousted U Nu who was heading a lively democracy in a land long denied self-government. South Korea suffered the same fate when the tradition of civilian supremacy was cast aside.

A Bill of Rights is, of course, no cure-all. Yet it is at times underrated. Some years ago it was said, "The due process clauses ought to go. It is highly significant that not a single constitution framed for English-speaking countries since the Fourteenth Amendment has embodied its provisions. And one would indeed be lacking in a sense of humor to suggest that life, liberty, or property is not amply protected in Canada, Australia, South Africa."[3] That was doubtless an accurate reflection at the time. Yet as things turned out the Republic of South Africa is an excellent contemporary example of the *in terrorem* influence of a lawmaking authority unrestrained by a Due Process Clause.

The provision in the Constitution of the Republic of South Africa that "The People of the Union acknowledge the sovereignty and the guidance of Almighty God" did not fulfill the need. Every time its courts construed a law to require equality in treatment of the races, the legislature enacted a law to wipe out the decision. It even created a High Court of Parliament to secure a reversal of a decision disliked by the government.[4] Elizabeth

Landis has shown how the South African legislature has salted *apartheid* or racial isolation into every aspect of life in that benighted realm.[5]

The experience in South Africa is modern proof of the importance of restraints on the legislative power. It underlines Bagehot's view that:

A legislative chamber is greedy and covetous; it acquires as much, it concedes as little as possible. The passions of its members are its rulers; the law-making faculty, the most comprehensive of the imperial faculties, is its instrument; it will *take* the administration if it can take it.[6]

South Africa in 1962 took the final step towards legislative supremacy by a new law governing "sabotage." Under that law (no. 76, 1962) such a broad sweep is given to offenses that racism can now reach almost any conduct; the defense of double jeopardy is practically abolished; the Minister of Justice by newspaper notice can ban a host of activities in the field of civil rights; and publication of the notice carries a conclusive presumption that the persons affected had knowledge of it. People are now banned from the country or closely confined; they are barred from attending meetings; their utterances cannot be published in South Africa nor in foreign papers brought into the country; and they are without remedy. They are without remedy because the penalties are imposed by the Minister of State concerned and his action cannot be upset by a court unless bad faith is shown. Moreover, the party whose liberties are restrained by the Minister has no right of hearing; and no evidence is placed before him for rebuttal or admission. That is to say, some of man's most highly prized personal rights are subject to administrative fiat; judicial review for all practical purposes is absent.

An independent judiciary construing and enforcing a Bill of Rights does not of course always have the final say. A judiciary —no matter how well insulated from popular pressures—could not withstand for long an executive or a legislative power that had the *consensus* of the nation behind it. Yet popular trends or mob passions might be checked at their inception and perhaps finally subdued if civil rights, enforced by an independent judiciary, were enshrined in a Bill of Rights.

It was for this reason that Madison emphasized the importance of a Bill of Rights:

1. The political truths declared in that solemn manner acquire by degrees the character of fundamental maxims of free Government, and as they become incorporated with the national sentiment, counteract the impulses of interest and passion. 2. Altho. it be generally true as above stated that the danger of oppression lies in the interested majorities of the people rather than in usurped acts of the Government, yet there may be occasions on which the evil may spring from the latter source; and on such, a bill of rights will be a good ground for an appeal to the sense of the community.[7]

We have ample proof, however, that ". . . a mere demarcation on parchment of the constitutional limits of the several departments, is not a sufficient guard against those encroachments which lead to a tyrannical concentration of all the powers of government in the same hands."[8]

Constitutions may be undone by erosion through judicial constructions. They are undone by timid popular protests when encroachments are first made on the liberty of a people. They are also undone by sudden convulsions in public affairs. As Madison said:

Should a Rebellion or insurrection alarm the people as well as the Government, and a suspension of the Hab. Corp. be dictated by the alarm, no written prohibitions on earth would prevent the measure.[9]

Yet the existence of a Bill of Rights may be not merely a rallying point; it may also become so much a way of life that no force can uproot it. This presupposes of course a *consensus* that the compact marks the limits of power as well as the source of it. That is to say, a Free Society requires a rule of law. Liberty under the law presupposes tolerance for differing views and, in time, the evolution of political parties that give expression and vitality to opposed schools of thought.

That condition, when it arrives, is the mark of a mature society. In communities where there is freedom of expression, in communities where the censor is not allowed to operate, ideas do not terrify and people can be educated for self-government. When ideas become too dangerous to discuss, when advocacy of an unpopular cause becomes a crime, timidity (with its companions, hate and fear) sets the mood of a people.

Development of tolerance for the opposition requires time and patience. It is not an instinct born in men. In the new countries, criticism of the leader is apt to be taken as a personal affront. Such was the failing of Menderes of Turkey. Fear of assassination often produces restraints compatible with dictatorship, not democracy. Moreover, once independence is achieved by a pastoral, underdeveloped nation, a leader rushing pell-mell toward industrialization may hold tight the reins of government. And where security is threatened by guerrilla activities, such as have preoccupied South Vietnam, the environment where dialogue and debate take the place of force does not develop.

Since we live on earth, not in Heaven, we will always be imperfect. Yet in spite of all obstacles, the creation of a Bill of Rights marks a start toward achieving a society where diversities in ideas, as well as race, can exist and flourish side by side. A Bill of Rights sets the ideal to which on occasion the people can be summoned. It is a reminder to officials that all power is a heady thing and that there are limits beyond which it is not safe to go.

A few provisions of our Bill of Rights, notably the Third Amendment and its prohibition against quartering of soldiers in private homes, have no immediate relation to any modern problem. Most of the other guarantees against government are, however, as important today as they were when first adopted. Many of them are even more important.

The Fourteenth and Fifteenth Amendments proclaim equality; and progress has been made toward that goal. But community after community still maintains and fosters in residential areas restrictive covenants against Jews and Negroes in spite of the fact that it would be unconstitutional for a court to enforce them. Racism is not peculiarly a problem of the South. Northern communities also practice it,[10] though the law denounces segregation in each of the fifty States.

Trade unions have been making progress in eliminating practices that discriminate against Negroes. Even so, one of the largest trade unions still maintains a racial barrier in its constitution. Moreover many unions—especially those in the construction industry—limit Negroes to servile jobs. Negroes indeed have a difficult time—not because of lack of talent but because of union practices—in rising to the level of skilled laborers. America has, however, come a long way since the Emancipation Proclamation—further as respects the race problem than any nation in a like period. Yet the disparity in income figures between Negro families on the one hand and white families on the other is a telling reminder of the regime of inequality, starting with education, that we have fostered over the decades. Even today there is not enough quiet evangelism afoot to increase the pace. Churches, schools, and the press are here and there vocal. But the overall community effort is not great. For example, how many real estate brokers in our metropolitan areas show disrespect for restrictive covenants?

When we move from the racial problem to other civil rights, we see another retreat. The Fifth Amendment is an example. One expects a street mob to be propelled by passion and use phrases such as "Fifth Amendment Communist." Legislative committees are perhaps the worst offenders. Witnesses are sometimes called in order to see how many times the Fifth Amendment will be invoked. The more times a witness invokes it, the guiltier he is—according to popular standards. Legislative committees are not the only offenders. It was a shocking experience for me to hear one of my former professors call another professor a "Fifth Amendment Communist." The intelligentsia are supposed to be the trustees of the values of the Free Society. They should know that the Fifth Amendment and its guarantee against compulsory self-incrimination have a long history, reflecting the need of the innocent as well as the guilty to be free from the coercion of government.

One who follows records of criminal cases in the courts knows that the third-degree method of exacting confessions—the modern inquisition—still prevails among the police. We boast that we are a government of laws, not of men; and we are indeed far advanced in that respect as compared with the Soviet system. Yet we too occasionally use Soviet methods. No one under our Constitution can be arrested except on probable cause. Unless the offender is apprehended in the act, a warrant must be obtained from the magistrate. Yet it is a notorious fact in the District of Columbia that there are thousands of "arrests for investigation" a year—a procedure the Soviets practice but one we abjure.

The right of privacy of which we boast is daily violated. Wiretapping is a notorious example. I reported in 1954 that New York City alone had 1,000 wiretaps a week. I was taken to task by prosecutors who proclaimed that the taps were in the hundreds for a whole year. So they were—when measured by the number of warrants issued by magistrates authorizing a wiretap. I had naively assumed that the New York police were law-abiding; but it later turned out that they were flouting New York law and tapping wires to their hearts' content.[11] Wiretapping is a mimic of an alien practice, where privacy gives way to a regime of constant surveillance.

The American system was designed as the system of the dialogue. Discourse and debate were to be unlimited. Government was never to lay a hand on a speaker to interrupt him or to punish him for what he believed and said. But the police have too often been on the side of the crowd rather than with the speaker. Instead of protecting him, they often haul him away when the crowd starts hooting.

DeTocqueville stated the philosophy of the First Amendment:

> If the absolute power of a majority were to be substituted by democratic nations for all the different powers that checked or retarded overmuch the energy of individual minds, the evils would only have changed character. Men would not have found the means of independent life; they would simply have discovered (no easy task) a new physiognomy of servitude. There is . . . here matter for profound reflection to those who look on freedom of thought as a holy thing and who hate not only the despot, but despotism. For myself, when I feel the hand of power lie heavy on my brow, I care but little to know who oppresses me; and I am not the more disposed to pass beneath the yoke because it is held out to me by the arms of a million men.[12]

Communist regimes punish speech. Next to a middleman making a profit, free speech is the worst crime. The Communists are true to their standards in condemning free speech, for nothing is more dangerous than an idea and its expression. A regimented society must control speech if people are to be subdued. The legal device for criticism of government in those countries is usually the word "instigate," with punishment accruing to anyone who expresses a hostile view. For anyone "disseminating" such a view, whether through newspapers, films, radio, or television, a longer prison term is imposed.[13] In Russia, the phrase "counter-revolutionary" is used in much the same way. We have used a different word, "advocate." But the method of control is similar. The Communists run true to form when they repress speech to discourage ideological strays. We forsake our ideal when we do the same.

The press is "free" in this country; and it has acquired vast business interests under the protection of the First Amendment. No censor sits at the editorial or news desk, as in either China or Formosa. Government places no hand on a publisher's shoulder for expressing views on any issue. Even the newspaper, however, is not "free" in a practical sense. Where one paper has a monopoly in an area, it seldom presents two sides of an issue. It too often hammers away on one ideological or political line using its monopoly position not to educate people, not to promote debate, but to inculcate in its readers one philosophy, one attitude—and to make money.

The press has frequently sounded the hue and cry against the unorthodox when it should have been educating the people on the values of the First, the Fourth, and the Fifth Amendments. The press during the days of the witch hunt helped make spectacles out of the heresy trials that took place before legislative committees. One can count on the fingers of two hands the papers that stood resolutely against the reign of terror during the '40's.

The exceptions are heartening. In 1961, a law professor from another state told the Minnesota police how to get around the law that requires prompt arraignment of a person arrested:

Wait till the judge goes home early on a Friday; then take the suspect into custody and you've got the whole weekend.

The Minneapolis Star—to its eternal credit—properly denounced this advice and proclaimed in favor of prompt arraignment as "the great legal tradition of free societies."[14]

An editorial broadcast recently stated:

. . . the newspaper decline has encouraged conformity. It is probably true that the newspaper proprietor with little or no competition in his own field tends to avoid extreme partisanship. But it is also true that, with some notable exceptions, newspaper editorial pages shy away from controversy, adopt the 'safe' position, and are tepid and uninspired.

That may explain, in part, the renewed popularity of some of the small magazines which deal in opinion, frequently unpopular opinion. And, if we may say so, the situation is also an excellent reason for vigorous editorializing by the nation's television and radio stations. The citizens of this country can make informed judgments on public questions only if they are exposed to contrasting points of view. Newspapers once performed this function almost alone. They are no longer able to do so. The vacuum that has been created will have to be filled.

Radio and TV stations often fear their advertisers who in turn fear non-conformists. Merchandising seems to become the "pursuit of happiness." So everything is subordinated to that end. Thus an actor who joins an anti-nuclear club is dropped because some might associate the sponsor with that cause and stop purchasing its hair oil or cosmetics. Another reason for increasing conformity in attitudes is traceable to the technology of modern communications of views, particularly broadcasting. Those media reach their greatest efficiency when they reach the largest possible audience. As Dan Lacy says, "This technological fact predisposes all the mass media to conform to an already widely accepted taste."[15] "The consequence is to press majority toward unanimity and to reinforce existing tastes and views with their own constant and amplified echo."[16] Now that Telstar has been launched and a worldwide communications system is at hand will the pressure be on to carry to the world not the healthy dissensions of a democracy but the new and deadening patterns of conformity?

To return to newspapers, their situation has changed greatly during the century since deTocqueville wrote:

The facility with which newspapers can be established produces a multitude of them; but as the competition prevents any considerable profit, persons of much capacity are rarely led to enagage in these undertakings. Such is the number of the public prints that even if they were a source of wealth, writers of ability could not be found to direct them all. The journalists of the United States are generally in a very humble position, with a scanty education and a vulgar turn of mind.[17]

The position of the modern media of communication is now vastly different. Today the combined ownership of papers and broadcasting stations means that any opportunity to develop a clash of ideas on important public issues never arises. Competitors have little chance to establish themselves. Only a group with many millions can start afresh in the newspaper field. Radio and TV licenses are closely rationed.

The newspapers that give a variety of views and news that is not slanted or contrived are few indeed. And the problem promises to get worse rather than better, as the number of English language newspapers continues to decrease, as shown by the following figures:

	Dailies	*Weeklies*
1941	1,998	10,796
1951	1,890	9,727
1961	1,850	8,953[18]

The press is not alone in contributing to the decline in freedom of expression. The church has not served its traditional educational role in the realm of civil rights. It has often reflected timid attitudes. Our churchmen have at times been worse than timid. The Catholic Bishops who threatened parishioners with excommunication unless they voted a certain way in the Puerto Rican elections committed the gravest sin of all, if sin can be measured by constitutional standards. While the Catholic clergy have been among the leaders in promoting the desegregation of the schools, other theologians have stayed strangely silent allowing the impression to grow that the whites occupy a preferred position in the Christian religion.

A word as to the lawyers. In 1770 British soldiers were tried in Boston for killing Americans in an episode known as the "Boston Massacre." John Adams and Josiah Quincy, Jr., defended them, six being acquitted and two being convicted of manslaughter. Feelings ran high. But Adams and Quincy did not hesitate, Adams saying that counsel "ought to be the very last thing that an accused Person should want in a free Country."[19] This was in the best tradition of our Bar. In American history lawyers have often rallied opinion outside of courtrooms in support of the despised minorities. Charles Evans Hughes, William E. Borah, and John W. Davis served in that role. A few lawyers still speak in that tradition. But most lawyers have remained silent.

There have not been many legislators in the '40's, '50's and '60's who have performed the role of a LaFollette or a George Norris and spoken out for the conscience of America. There have been few pulpits, few boards of education, few parent-teachers associations to protest against the rash of loyalty oaths with which we have been afflicted. When the numbers are counted across the land, the ranks are thin.

The affluent society is not apt to produce defenders of the unorthodox. Whitney Griswold, President of Yale, recently said:

We have become too much a nation of lookers and listeners, a nation of spectators. Amidst the easy artificiality of our life, the plethora of substitutes for learning and thinking, the innumerable devices for avoiding or delegating personal responsibility for our opinions, even for having any opinions, the fine edge of our faith has been dulled, our creative powers atrophied.

The big bureaucracies of government, of business, and of trade unions tend to produce men and women who walk in unison.

When a sense of insecurity pervades the nation, the price paid for liberty may seem to be too high.

When the courts give away, the default is apt to be complete.

II.

The default of the judiciary, as respects the Bill of Rights, has not been purposeful and it is not of recent origin. Its beginnings are distant from the contemporary scene. The retreat has had two manifestations. First, the Courts have diluted the specific commands of the Constitution. Parts of the Constitution are generalized, such as the provisions of the Fifth and Fourteenth Amendments that no person shall be deprived of life, liberty, or property "without due process of law." Parts contain partial prohibitions, such as those against "unreasonable" searches and seizures in the Fourth Amendment and "excessive" bail in the Eighth. Others are in the form of commands, such as "Congress shall make no law . . . abridging the freedom of speech" in the First Amendment.

The guarantees that the Framers phrased in terms of commands with no qualifications would seem therefore to be in a "preferred" category. Yet even those guarantees that are seemingly "preferred" have by judicial construction been taken as only admonitions to moderation. The words "Congress shall make no law . . . abridging freedom of speech" have been read to mean "Congress may make some laws that abridge freedom of speech." This interpretation would be proper under the Indian Constitution which in Art. 19 (1)(a) says that all citizens shall have the right "to freedom of speech and expression" and in Art. 19 (2) says that such right does not prevent the state from imposing "reasonable restrictions on the exercise" of that right "in the interests of the security of the state, friendly relations with foreign states, public order, decency or morality or in relation to contempt of court, defamation or incitement to an offense."

Legislative supremacy, explicit in the Indian Constitution, is read into ours by judicial construction without any need for a constitutional amendment.

The requirement that a warrant be issued by a magistrate only on a showing of probable cause has been taken to mean that the police need no warrant to invade the privacy of a home, provided they come in uniforms of health inspectors.[20] The Fourth Amendment has also been read to permit the use of administrative search warrants (issued without a magistrate's approval in connection with civil proceedings) even when the evidence obtained is used in a criminal prosecution.[21]

The formal constitutional guarantee that bail will not be "excessive" presupposes the availability of bail.[22] Without bail, a person can be held until it is found convenient to release him.

Bail is designed to keep a person out of jail until found guilty (unless his release would be dangerous) and until he has had his appeal (unless he raises "frivolous" questions). The decision in *Carlson* v. *Landon*,[23] left the grant or denial of bail to aliens largely in the discretion of Congress—a situation that can bear heavily on unpopular minorities.

Agreement of a group to teach a political philosophy obnoxious to the majority, i.e., communism, becomes a criminal conspiracy punishable by fine and imprisonment.[24] Advocacy of the Communist creed, as distinguished from passive belief in it, was held punishable in *Scales* v. *United States*.[25] Our debate on how much belief in communism makes one a Communist has its counterpart in Russia. For there the same question is shown on the reverse side of the coin—how much of a democrat does one have to be in order to become counter-revolutionary.

Chafee said: "The First Amendment was written by men . . . who intended to wipe out the common law of sedition, and make further prosecutions for criticism of the government, without any incitement to lawbreaking, forever impossible in the United States . . ."[26] Others deny that premise.[27] The latter school in effect says that the Framers "spoke for unabridged freedom of speech and press but were consciously lying as they did so."[28] The votes have been against the Chafee position. Votes make the law but not necessarily the correct or the just law. The accounting of history will, I think, show that Chafee and Meiklejohn, not the modern apologists for the prevailing view, were right.

The Virginia Resolutions drafted by Madison, protesting the Alien and Sedition Acts, stated that the power to suppress freedom of expression was "a power which more than any other, ought to produce universal alarm, because it is levelled against the right of freely examining public characters and measures, and of free communication among the people thereon, which has ever been justly deemed the only effectual guardian of every other right."[29]

But Madison's views have not been honored and a rewriting of the Bill of Rights has taken place with the result that civil rights have been diluted.

The second default is in the refusal of the courts to apply the federal standard of Due Process to the States. The Bill of Rights, enacted as a restraint on the central government, gives both procedural and substantive content to the requirements of Due Process. When the Fourteenth Amendment was adopted and the requirements of Due Process were imposed upon the States, the normal assumption would have been that what was Due Process in the federal domain became Due Process in the domain of the States. The debates *pro* and *con* have been continuous. The results are well known. The majority view is that the standards of Due Process for the States are in part those for the Federal Government but only selectively so.

The First Amendment is said to be incorporated into the Due Process Clause of the Fourteenth Amendment. So are the Fourth Amendment, the Just Compensation Clause of the Fifth Amendment and a part of the Self-Incrimination Clause of the Fifth Amendment; and so are the right to a public trial, protection against cruel and unusual punishments, the right to be free of coerced confessions, and the right to counsel in the more serious criminal cases.[30] What justification can be made for this selective picking and choosing, bringing some guarantees into Due Process and leaving others out?

No convincing answer has yet been made to the position of the first Mr. Justice Harlan in *Hurtado* v. *California*,[31] that what is Due Process in terms of the Fifth Amendment should be Due Process in terms of the Fourteenth.

Due Process, to use the vernacular, is the wild card that can be put to such use as the judges choose. Those who use it as the wild card often deny doing so, saying that Due Process is not subjective, that it has its roots in civilized ideas of ordered liberty. Yet no matter what the judges say, Due Process, as it is presently employed, is fickle and capricious. Its highly subjective and personal character is illustrated by *Rochin* v. *California*,[32] holding that evidence obtained by forceable use of a stomach pump on a suspect violates Due Process, and by *Breithaupt* v. *Abram*,[33] holding that evidence obtained by taking blood from an unconscious person does not.

The words Due Process are "so undefined, either by their intrinsic meaning, or by history, or by tradition, that they leave the individual Justice free, if indeed they do not actually compel him, to fill in the vacuum with his own controlling notions of economic, social, and industrial facts with reference to which they are invoked. These judicial judgments are thus bound to be determined by the experience, the environment, the fears, the imagination, of the different Justices."[34]

While constitutional barricades have been lowered, this was not done by officials who were opposed to the Free Society. Their conception of the Free Society is one where the legislature is relatively supreme. Specific guarantees, in their view, are in the keeping of the lawmakers and, no matter how absolute in terms, are not commands or restraints that fence off certain domains from governmental action.

What Marshall wrote in *Fletcher* v. *Peck* has been largely forgotten:

> Whatever respect might have been felt for the state sovereignties, it is not to be disguised, that the framers of the constitution viewed, with some apprehension, the violent acts which might grow out of the feelings of the moment; and that the people of the United States, in adopting that instrument, have manifested a determination to shield themselves and their property from the effects of those sudden and strong passions to which men are exposed. The restrictions on the legislative power of the states are obviously founded in this sentiment; and the constitution of the United States contains what may be deemed a bill of rights for the people of each state.[35]

Jefferson, who did not always agree with Marshall, shared the foregoing sentiments. Jefferson, in a letter to Madison, March 15, 1789, emphasizing the importance of a Bill of Rights, said: "The tyranny of the legislatures is the most formidable dread at present, and will be for long years."[36]

Judge-made rules have also contributed to the decline in civil rights. Resort to courts for relief has been greatly circumscribed by a variety of devices.

Under our federal system—particularly in light of the Ninth and Tenth Amendments—federal courts fill a restricted role. They sit in judgment on state courts only as respects federal questions— a narrow jurisdiction that has obtained from the very beginning. That principle has many manifestations in our laws. Thus, Congress out of respect for state law enforcement wrote into a statute the requirements that no *federal* habeas corpus be entertained "unless it appears that the applicant has exhausted the remedies available in the courts of the State."[37] It was held in 1950 that state remedies are not exhausted, even though all are pursued to their end in the hierarchy of state courts, if denial of a remedy in the state courts was not sought to be corrected by certiorari to the Federal Supreme Court; and in that event, *federal* habeas corpus is not available.[38] Yet for years the Bar had, and has, been told— which is the truth—that denial of certiorari "imports no expression of opinion upon the merits of the case."[39] Thus a needless barrier—the performing of a ritual that has no significance— was placed in the path of the litigant seeking fedreal relief from unconstitutional procedures. To date, the requirement has been lifted only when the state remedy could not reach the federal claim, as where state *habeas corpus* is restricted to its ancient role of testing strictly jurisdictional defects.[40]

Other judge-made rules have added impediments to the administration of justice. In *Daniels* v. *Allen*,[41] relief in a seemingly meritorious case was denied in a *federal* habeas corpus case because the petitioner had failed to exhaust his state remedies. If he had had no counsel, if prison authorities had prevented him from perfecting an appeal, the defect would have been overlooked.[42] He had 60 days to appeal to the state supreme court and it was said he did not appeal in time. If he had mailed his notice of appeal on the 60th day, it would have been timely.[43] But since his lawyer delivered it on the 61st (when it would have been received had it been mailed on the 60th day) his state appeal was held untimely. Therefore he was barred from getting federal relief on a claim that seemed to be meritorious. Thus are judge-made rules raised as barricades that block all paths—both state and federal—to Due Process.

The abstention doctrine is another judge-made rule that has served to blunt the edges of many laws, including those governing civil rights. By reason of that doctrine effective judicial relief has often become too remote and expensive for all except those with a long purse or those who can take the costs of litigation as tax deductions. The relation between federal and state agencies is of course fraught with difficulties under a federal regime. But those who go to a federal court to vindicate a federal right are there as a matter of right.[44] Yet they are often denied a prompt decision[45] being remitted instead to state courts where they must start long drawn-out and expensive litigation in tribunals which at times are hostile to the claim of federal right. The result has been to relegate the federal courts to a secondary role in situations where, by reason of their versatility in federal constitutional law, they should carry the burden.[46]

Another judge-made rule that involves the so-called "political" question was taken over from English law and put to new uses under our constitutional form of government. Some of the cases involve instances where a court properly refuses to command an executive officer to exercise his discretion one way or the other. They are cases, in other words, where no court could compel the exercise of the discretion without taking over the office—which of course no court should do.

Another group concerns functions specifically assigned by the Constitution to a particular department. Treaty-making authority is one example. The power to conduct foreign affairs, including the decision to recognize or not to recognize a particular regime, is another.

Yet even though power is given exclusively to one department to do a certain act, when the power is exercised, justiciable rights may arise. Private rights commonly derive from treaties. The Chief Executive, as Commander-in-Chief, makes decisions in which no one else can participate. But what he does often gives rise to claims that courts should adjudicate.

Chicago & Southern Air Lines, Inc. v. *Waterman S.S. Corp.*,[47] held that since the grant of certificates for overseas airline service is subject to the President's approval, even the question whether statutory standards had been satisfied was "political" and beyond the competence of the court to adjudicate. The reason is difficult to understand.

Pacific States Tel. & Tel. Co. v. *Oregon*,[48] involved the constitutionality of the use of the initiative and referendum. Suit was brought to enforce a tax assessment made by a state, the defense being that the law was unconstitutional because it was the product of the initiative and referendum. The case was dismissed because, the Court said, it involved a "political" question. The defense seems frivolous; yet why the issue was not justiciable is a mystery.

Although Article 4, Section 4, of the Constitution provides that "The United States shall guarantee to every state in this union a republican form of government," it has been held over and again that the enforcement of the guarantee is beyond the competence of the courts. The reason is also a mystery. *Luther* v. *Borden*,[49] involved the legality of an arrest, which is conventional material for courts to determine. The underlying issues which the Court said were "political" involved first, the right of people to vote which has long been subject to judicial cognizance and second, the validity of a regime of martial law. The latter too has been repeatedly subject to review in the courts as the landmark case of *Sterling* v. *Constantin*,[50] shows. The Court should have said in *Luther* v. *Borden* what Chief Justice Holt said in *Ashby* v. *White* respecting damages for failure to let a citizen vote:

This is a matter of property determinable before us. Was ever such a petition heard of in Parliament, as that a man was hindered of giving his vote, and praying them to give him remedy? The Parliament undoubtedly would say, take your remedy at law. It is not like the case of determining the right of election between the candidates.[51]

Georgia v. *Stanton*[52] marked an extension of the domain of the "political" question. The Court refused to intervene in a suit to enjoin the Secretary of War from taking over the government of Georgia under the notorious Reconstruction Acts. Conflicts between federal officers and States have been frequent in our history. *Georgia* v. *Stanton* seems to mean that the more serious the damage to the State, the less available a judicial remedy. It also runs counter to the western tradition that the civilian authority is supreme over the military.[53]

It was in the tradition of civilian supremacy that the courts reviewed the actions of the military in removing citizens of Japanese ancestry from the West Coast during World War II. Those decisions,[54] while arguably right in not overruling the military on its appraisal of the likelihood that the Japanese army might land on the West Coast, seem, in retrospect, to be wrong in letting the military remove those citizens *via* concentration centers.

The judiciary plainly has a restricted role. It does not fashion policies. It should not try to occupy the office of the executive, the legislature, or the administrative. But once a "case" or "controversy" arises, the issue should be subject to adjudication in a court, unless the subject matter has been wholly and indivisibly entrusted by the Constitution to another branch.[55] It is becoming more and more apparent, as our affairs become more and more complicated, that absent a judicial remedy for a wrong, there will be none within the reach of the average person. It may be unwise or impractical to try to formulate a decree in some cases. But the "political" question should no longer be used as a thicket behind which the judiciary retreats.

The Court reclaimed some of the ground lost when it held that reapportionment is not a "political" question over which the judiciary has no control. I speak of course of *Baker v. Carr,*[56] where without judicial remedies the "rotten boroughs" would continue for years on end.

The judicial construction of the words "cases" or "controversies" in Article III of the Constitution excludes "abstract questions" and questions not ripe for review. The result, while sound in theory, has been a refusal of the courts to resolve many vivid controversies. Risks, uncertainties, and doubts that give rise to insecurity—these are certainly proper for judicial decision. The declaratory judgment is, indeed, based on that theory, though it is, of course, subject to the constitutional requirement that there be a "case" or "controversy."[57] Yet clashes that are real by standards of the workaday world are often not adequately devastating to satisfy the courts.

Civil Service Rules prohibit those holding positions in the competitive classified service from taking "active part in political management or in political campaigns." Certain workers, holding such positions, sought a declaratory judgment ruling that the Rules were invalid, saying that they wished to engage in those kinds of activities as private citizens and on their own time but that, if they did so, the Rules would make them subject to dismissal. Though doing the acts in question would have imperiled the employees' status and jobs, the Court held there was no justiciable controversy.[58] Few people are so financially independent that they can risk their job to enjoy their constitutional rights.

Standing to sue is a matter with which the legislature has sometimes dealt. Laws have at times depended on the informer for law enforcement[59] as the *qui tam* cases illustrate.[60] Congress has given judicial review of agency decisions to any person "suffering legal wrong" or "adversely affected" or "aggrieved" by agency action[61]—a law which at an early stage was vetoed on the ground that this intrusion of the judiciary into administrative affairs would be a setback for reform measures.[62] Yet the passage of time has indicated that more, rather than less, review is essential for responsible administrative action, not because the courts in fact materially curb the administrative process but because the prospect of judicial review makes administrative action more meticulous and conscientious. While Congress cannot, of course, expand the constitutional definition of "case" or "controversy," it has broad authority to determine who has standing to protest the action of administrative agencies.[63] When this authority was extended to private parties to vindicate public rights, they were appropriately called "private Attorney Generals" by the late Jerome Frank.[64] But overall the courts have not been hospitable to the idea.

The lack of standing to sue has often been used to keep the judicial door closed, except and unless a person is about to be hung or the law in some other tangible way has fastened its claws on him. A large consumer of coal was held to have no standing to challenge price-fixing orders of a federal agency.[65] Even ruin of a private business by a public enterprise did not give a private party standing to challenge the constitutionality of the public project.[66] Laws may make the giving of birth control advice by doctors a crime; yet the doctor must risk fine or imprisonment before he can drive the cloud of that unconstitutional law from his practice.[67]

Taxpayers have no standing to challenge federal laws making appropriations. The relation of a municipal taxpayer to the expenditure of funds by the municipality is said to be "direct and immediate and the remedy by injunction to prevent their misuse is not inappropriate."[68] The relation of a taxpayer of the United States to the Federal Government, however, is said to be "very different" because his interest "in the moneys of the Treasury" is "shared with millions of others; is comparatively minute and indeterminable; and the effect upon future taxation, of any payment out of the funds, so remote, fluctuating and uncertain, that no basis is afforded for an appeal to the preventive powers of a court of equity."[69] Thus it is concluded that the constitutionality of a federal appropriation is "essentially a matter of public and not of individual concern."[70]

The result is that no matter how massive the public injury may be, as for example the making of large appropriations to religious schools, no judicial remedy is available to the taxpayers. An extreme application of this rule was made in *Doremus* v. *Board of Education*.[71] That was a suit by parents and taxpayers in the New Jersey courts to declare invalid a state statute which provided for the reading, without comment, of five verses of the Old Testament at the opening of each public school day. The parents did not want their children exposed to the teachings of the Old Testament. The taxpayers did not want school facilities, financed by public funds, used on such a religious venture. While the New Jersey courts gave the plaintiff standing to sue, the Supreme Court held otherwise and dismissed the appeal. The child of the parents involved had graduated before the appeal could reach the court, and so as to them the case was moot. Yet the taxpayers' suit was held not to be a "good-faith pocketbook action."[72]

It seems plain that if the claim of the taxpayers was correct and the First Amendment was being violated, taxes were being deflected from the constitutional purposes for which they were paid. All of the taxpayers in the town certainly would have standing to sue, for no others would have a greater interest. The fact that the interests of the individual taxpayers were small did not make the suit any the less real, substantial, and vital to the parties.

Everson v. *Board of Education*[73]—a case started in the state courts and decided by the Supreme Court on the merits—was a taxpayer's suit to enjoin a board of education from using public funds to furnish transportation to students attending parochial schools. If *Everson* is right in noting jurisdiction, *Doremus* is wrong. The two cannot stand together, unless the law is to be capricious. It is possible to say, as in *Everson*, that First Amendment rights are by nature of the constitutional command so *preferred* that taxpayers should be given standing to protect them, and that the more vague, generalized rights of Due Process involved in other cases require that one who makes the challenge have a more specific, tangible interest at stake. Where a constitutional right is, by the place the Framers gave it in the hierarchy, a *preferred* right, standing to sue to vindicate it should be readily granted. That distinction could explain the difference between *Everson* and *Frothingham* but not between *Everson* and *Doremus*. Judicial rules are, indeed, often designed to protect *preferred* constitutional rights, though there can be no satisfactory reconciliation of all the cases. That rationale will explain many of the cases involving racial discrimination.[74] And it also explains *Truax* v. *Raich*,[75] where a law, discriminatory against aliens but enforceable only against employers, was allowed to be challenged by an alien-employee.

This is not a novel drawing of lines. It was recently said that "the doctrine of unconstitutional indefiniteness has been used by the Supreme Court almost invariably for the creation of an insulating buffer zone of added protection at the peripheries of several of the Bill of Rights freedoms."[76] That view has support in some cases: "So vague and indeterminate are the boundaries thus set to the freedom of speech and assembly that the law necessarily violates the guarantees of liberty embodied in the Fourteenth Amendment."[77]

Kin to these cases are those holding that even though the police power is adequate to reach disorder and other physical conduct on the periphery of First Amendment rights, such laws must be narrowly drawn to meet the precise evil, lest they trench on constitutional guarantees.[78]

The cases on standing to sue show that the federal courts in general have been inhospitable to the adjudication of constitutional questions. That reluctance, when added to the watered-down version of the Bill of Rights that we now have, explains the ascendancy of legislative power and the decline of judicial authority. A Karl Llewellyn would call these rationalizations "the balm and smugness" which bait the "invertebrates among us."

It is often said that judicial intrusion should be infrequent, since it is "always attended with a serious evil, namely, that the correction of legislative mistakes comes from the outside, and the people thus lose the political experience, and the moral education and stimulus that come from fighting the question out in the ordinary way, and correcting their own errors"; that the effect of a participation by the judiciary in these processes is "to dwarf the political capacity of the people, and to deaden its sense of moral responsibility."[79]

Yet the judiciary is an indispensable part of the operation of our federal system. With the growing complexities of government it is often the one and only place where effective relief can be obtained. If the judiciary were to become a super-legislative group sitting in judgment on the affairs of the people, the situation would be intolerable. But where wrongs to individuals are done by violation of specific guarantees, it is abdication for courts to close their doors. That retreat has been applauded by those who think that if the judiciary were more alert "Congress would soon have enough of such 'fairness.'"[80] This view is degrading to the legislative branch—implying that it has no respect for the constitutional tradition of *Marbury* v. *Madison*.[81] The appellate jurisdiction of the Court, as well as the entire fabric of the lower federal court system, is left by the Constitution to Congress. Congress once was propelled by the passions of the day to withdraw one category of jurisdiction from the Court.[82] But the episode was a minor one in our constitutional history.

In the 1950's and early 1960's there were bills introduced in Congress to deny the court power to review certain types of cases, e.g., the jurisdiction of legislative committees where a witness was charged with contempt; federal or state statutes or administrative orders dealing with "subversive" activities; state administration of its public school system; laws of the States regulating admission of lawyers; and state laws challenged on the ground that they conflict with a federal law, unless the federal law contains an express provision that it excludes all state laws on the subject. Proposals have been made that no state law shall be held unconstitutional except on the concurrence of all participating Justices; and that a hearing be granted the parties before any judgment is modified, affirmed, reversed, vacated, or set aside. Some have offered measures that would make decisions of the Court changeable only by legislative enactments or constitutional amendments. A bill was offered to make issuance of writs of certiorari possible only on a vote of five Justices, four being the number presently required. But at no time has Congress altered basically or fundamentally the Court's appellate jurisdiction. It has adhered to the decision of the First Congress which gave the Court power to reverse or affirm cases coming from state courts in which was involved either a decision adverse to the validity of an Act of Congress or a decision upholding a state law challenged on federal grounds.

DeTocqueville traced the manner in which the influence of legal habits extends throughout the entire American system "so that at last the whole people contract the habits and the tastes of the judicial magistrate."[83] The American people are more mature in their acceptance of a regime of law than the timid, doctrinaire spokesmen against the use of judicial power are apparently aware.

The words of Marshall in *Marbury* v. *Madison* announcing the duty of courts to refuse to fasten unconstitutional laws on the people need repeating:

> If an act of the legislature, repugnant to the constitution, is void, does it, notwithstanding its invalidity, bind the courts, and oblige them to give it effect? Or, in other words, though it be not law, does it constitute a rule as operative as if it was a law? This would be to

overthrow, in fact, what was established in theory; and would seem, at first view, an absurdity too gross to be insisted on. It shall, however, receive a more attentive consideration.

It is, emphatically, the province and duty of the judicial department, to say what the law is. Those who apply the rule to particular cases, must of necessity expound and interpret that rule. If two laws conflict with each other, the courts must decide on the operation of each. So, if a law be in opposition to the constitution; if both the law and the constitution apply to a particular case, so that the court must either decide that case, conformable to the law, disregarding the constitution; or conformable to the constitution, disregarding the law; the court must determine which of these conflicting rules governs the case: this is of the very essence of judicial duty. If then, the courts are to regard the constitution, and the constitution is superior to any ordinary act of the legislature, the constitution, and not such ordinary act, must govern the case to which they both apply.

Those men, who controvert the principle, that the constitution is to be considered, in court, as a paramount law, are reduced to the necessity of maintaining that courts must close their eyes on the constitution, and see only the law. This doctrine would subvert the very foundation of all written constitutions. It would declare that an act which, according to the principles and theory of our government, is entirely void, is yet, in practice, completely obligatory. It would declare, that if the legislature shall do what is expressly forbidden, such act, notwithstanding the express prohibition, is in reality effectual. It would be giving to the legislature a practical and real omnipotence, with the same breath which professes to restrict their powers within narrow limits. It is prescribing limits, and declaring that those limits may be passed at pleasure. That it thus reduces to nothing, what we have deemed the greatest improvement on political institutions, a written constitution, would, of itself, be sufficient, in America, where written constitutions have been viewed with so much reverence, for rejecting the construction. But the peculiar expressions of the constitution of the United States furnish additional arguments in favour of its rejection.[84]

Unlike the British system, ours depends for its competence on three departments of government, each fulfilling the special role assigned to it by the Constitution.

We have a Bill of Rights designed to keep government out of private domains. But the fences have been broken down; and machinery to restore them has been denied. The Bill of Rights—with the judicial gloss it has acquired—plainly is not adequate to protect the individual against the growing bureaucracy. He faces a formidable opponent in government, even when he is endowed with funds and with courage. The individual is almost certain to be plowed under, unless he has a well-organized active political group to speak for him. The church is one. The press is another. The union is a third. But if a powerful sponsor is lacking, individual liberty withers—in spite of glowing opinions and resounding constitutional phrases.

Chief Justice Hughes, writing in *The Supreme Court of the United States*[85] spoke of the Court's "self-inflicted wounds." His examples were three in number.[86] One was *Hepburn* v. *Griswold*,[87] and *Knox* v. *Lee*,[88] where the Court, on a reargument before a full Bench, held the legal tender acts constitutional, reversing its earlier decision. The second involved the *Income Tax Cases*[89] where on reargument before a full Bench and a change in one Justice's vote, the federal act was declared unconstitutional. These decisions aroused public opinion. Yet whether the decisions were right or wrong, it is the role of the judiciary to make pronouncements on constitutional issues, whatever the climate of public opinion. Short range changes in constitutional doctrine are not unusual, either as a result of a change in the Bench[90] or a change in the views of the Justices themselves.[91] And either seems a more honorable, a more frank course than failure to speak up or the announcement of a constitutional doctrine that a majority disapproves.

These short-range changes in constitutional law are indeed less disturbing than the changes made by *Erie R.R.* v. *Tompkins*,[92] when Justice Brandeis wrote the opinion in which Chief Justice Hughes joined and which overruled a ninety-year old constitutional precedent.

Yet none of these, in my view, was a "self-inflicted wound." Rather they represent responsible judicial management of constitutional issues, whatever one's views of the merits might be.

The *Dred Scott* case,[93] the third example cited by Hughes, involved a different situation. As Mr. Justice Curtis stated in his dissent,[94] once the Court decided that the federal courts had no jurisdiction over the controversy, it transcended "the limits of the authority of the court" to go on and render an opinion on the large issues of the power of Congress to regulate slavery. The opinions in the *Dred Scott* case are indeed filled with dicta. No one reveres the case as a precedent, for it was wrong on the merits, as Lincoln made clear. But it is not unusual for a court to indulge in dictum. In *Matter of Kentucky* v. *Dennison*,[95] the Court made broad rulings as to the duty of a Governor to allow a prisoner to be extradited by another State under a federal statute, but ruled it had no power to compel it. The much revered opinion of Marshall in *Marbury* v. *Madison*[96] first decided that Marbury's commission had been wrongfully withheld as he had been lawfully appointed to a federal office and then held that the Court had no jurisdiction to do anything about it.

The real "self-inflicted" wounds are those occasioned when judges refuse to act.

In the practical world uncertainties may be as debilitating as actual restraints; clouds on title may be created by fears of enforcement, as well as by actual criminal or other proceedings. The decisions dealing with those problems do not follow a straight line. They show indeed many inconsistencies. In general the federal decisions lean heavily on the side of a denial of judicial relief, which means that the individual is left more and more to political processes to vindicate his rights. But that form of relief is more and more ineffective, as our bureaucracy increases and the complexities of life multiply. What can an individual do but bow to the bureaucracy if a court gives him no standing to sue? Only the most powerful lobbies can reverse a trend these days. Getting a Congress to reverse itself is or may be no more difficult than getting a change in an administrative directive. The more realistic approach was stated by the Supreme Court of Missouri:

> The fact that in this case the city was not prepared, because of failure to appropriate funds, to enforce the ordinance when this action was filed, or that plaintiffs had not then actually violated the restrictions of the ordinance does not make this action premature. The ordinance had been duly adopted. It was a law affecting the plaintiffs. The plaintiffs must assume the city will enforce its laws.[97]

The citizen should know that in the courts one can get justice, no matter how discriminatory government officials may be. When the judiciary is no longer "the great rock" in the storm, as Lord Sankey once put it, when the courts are niggardly in the use of their power and reach great issues only timidly and reluctantly, the force of the Bill of Rights in the life of the nation is greatly weakened.

Gideon Hausner, after reviewing the severe security measures sometimes needed for Israel's survival and the vigilance of her courts in maintaining the rights of individuals, recently stated, "When all is said and done, one is inclined to think that a rigid constitutional frame is on the whole preferable even if it serves no better purpose than obstructing and embarrassing an overactive Executive."[98]

III

Our ideas of liberty or freedom are contained in the main in two commands of the Bill of Rights: first, the things government may not do; and second, the procedures government must follow in case it takes certain proceedings against the individual. That is to say, they fence government in as respects some matters and in others provide procedural safeguards for the individual in case government brings its awesome power to bear against him.

So far as the Bill of Rights is concerned, the individual is on his own when it comes to the pursuit of happiness. The right to work, the right to education, the right to marry as one chooses, the right to medical care—these and all like guarantees are significantly absent. The closest the Framers came to the *affirmative* side of liberty was in "the right of the people to bear arms." Yet this too has been greatly modified by judicial construction.

In the beginning, many colonists, particularly in Massachusetts, believed that government in America, like some existing Moslem regimes, ought to have certain specified religious ends in view: the salvation of men's souls, the maintenance of the church, and the preservation of godliness through laws penalizing heresy or absence from church services, or the doing of certain acts on the Sabbath. The present popular conception of democracy did not arrive on these shores full-blown, as the Handlins in *The Dimensions of Liberty* show.[99] John Cotton wrote in 1636 of democracy in disparaging words:

> Democracy, I do not conceyve that ever God did ordeyne as a fitt government eyther for church or commonwealth. If the people be governors, who shall be governed? As for monarchy, and aristocracy, they are both of them clearly approoved, and directed in scripture, yet so as referreth the soveraigntie to himselfe, and setteth up Theocracy in both, as the best forme of government in the commonwealth, as well as in the church.[100]

When the Constitution and the Bill of Rights were adopted and the new American federation launched, the state became the arbiter, letting the individual (or more particularly free enterprise) go unrestrained except when extreme limits of conduct were reached. The shift from that regime to the welfare state was slow and gradual. The transition was at first impeded by the judiciary. The Due Process Clause of the Fourteenth Amendment was used to annul state legislation; and the Commerce Clause was construed restrictively to curtail the power of Congress. But those two barriers were in time removed and the welfare state became constitutionally possible and increasingly attractive from a political viewpoint.

But the welfare state is a side issue. The central problem of the age is the scientific revolution and all the wonders and the damage it brings. The scientific revolution has created new centers of power in those who finance, it *viz.* federal officials or more particularly, the Pentagon and the Atomic Energy Commission. The autonomy of universities is threatened, as Carl F. Stover points out in *The Government of Science.*[101]

The scientific revolution produces increasing crop surpluses.

The scientific revolution produces a high-level technology that requires more and more controls, which in turn mean more and more government.

The scientific revolution displaces men and substitutes the machine with the result that we have the promise of a permanent surplus of unemployed people.

The liberal-conservative dichotomy of the 1930's is obsolete. What are the rights of men against the machine as it becomes increasingly important? What do we substitute for work—as a discipline, and as a means of distributing income? What Bill of Rights does man now need to keep a modicum of liberty? The forces allied against the individual have never been greater. The scientific revolution makes production and consumption the ends of society. Yet are they "the pursuit of happiness?" The scientific revolution teaches conformity in a myriad of ways. The scientific revolution produces, indeed, a vast interdependency among people. Where in this tightly knit regime is man to find liberty?

The scientific revolution turns out more and more experts who govern a nation's fate. Who can stand up against the word of the expert? Who can defy the expert? A specialty, like science and law, often produces narrow-minded people. Chemical companies endow universities with chairs and scholarships that produce entomologists with the chemical-company point of view. The expert who knows how to use a pesticide is like the medical specialist who knows the heart, the liver, or the joints but not the whole person. Each specialist has such a narrow view that the wholeness of the problem escapes him. People become statistics and eventually the victims of the experts.

A society of the dialogue would expose the fallacies of the experts and show that, while certain detergents were wondrous aids to the housewife, they are insolubles that eventually poison even our percolating waters and artesian wells. A society of the dialogue would be up in arms over the use of insecticides and over the destruction of our wilderness areas by modern Genghis Khans, both in and out of government. But the society of the dialogue seems to be on the decline; and individuals have less and less recourse to any corrective remedy against those who hold positions of power.

That is why the need for procedural due process is even greater today than in 1789, when the Bill of Rights was adopted. If the Bill of Rights were being written today, it certainly would provide people with protection against poisoning by insecticides— one of America's acute problems, as Rachel Carson shows in her book *Silent Spring*.[102] If the Bill of Rights were being written today, it also would encompass some of the recurring evils arising out of the vast exercise of authority through the administrative agency. Thus in one State an administrative board of three may, on a majority vote, sterilize a person without notice, without an opportunity to be heard, without an application being made to any other tribunal or agency. One State provides that a patient in a state hospital—certified as being "mentally ill" and who has previously committed a crime—may be transferred without any hearing to a hospital for the criminally insane.[103] A business recently was abolished by a Board of Health through an amendment of its Rules that was made without notice or opportunity to be heard even by the business in question. A wilderness area may be destroyed by the *fiat* of a few men in the Forestry Service through spraying, or logging, or road building. The

THE BILL OF RIGHTS IS NOT ENOUGH

Bureau of Land Management fences people out of public lands and gets money from Congress to do so—all for the benefit of a few ranchers and to the certain disaster of the antelope who must migrate and yet who cannot jump fences. Here again people lose their inheritance without notice, without hearing, or without the need of the agency to obtain prior approval from another tribunal.

Moreover, traditional ideas of Due Process are not enough to put into harness the modern administrative agency, let alone the modern prosecutor, or the modern legislative committee.

The power of the military to control its posts, subjects civilians who work there to unreviewable ideological supervision.[104] Matters that jeopardize a person's job[105] can be adjudicated without the time-honored safeguard of the right of confrontation.[106] The Armed Forces are allowed to downgrade a doctor because of his insistence on his constitutional rights.[107]

It has been said that there is nothing in the Magna Carta "which ought to exclude the best ideas of all systems and of every age," and that "the new and various experiences of our own situation and system will mould and shape it into new and not less useful forms."[108] Those ideas represent a progressive approach to law. Over the years, however, the judiciary has not been the central force in establishing or maintaining civil rights. There have been exceptions as in the evolution of the writ of habeas corpus—notably Chief Justice Vaughn's action in *Bushell's Case*,[109] when he released from jail the jury that had acquitted William Penn of disturbing the peace. There has been much judicial creativeness shown in the evolution of the common law, Cardozo's ruling in *MacPherson* v. *Buick Motor Co.*[110] being but one of many examples. Mansfield's decision in the *Somerset* case[111] that a slave who set foot on British soil became free was a golden day for justice. There are of course many others in the tradition that Karl Llewellyn called "the Grand Style of Reason."[112]

Normally, however, judges have a bramble bush which they call the law and behind which they stay. They profess that it confines them and prevents them from doing justice. There is indeed a naive idea that *justice* has no place in the operation of federalism, that *law* supplies the only criteria. But *justice* often supplies the criterion in federalism. For a long time some States denied an impecunious defendant a lawyer in a criminal case. An exception was created in capital and in other more serious cases. For then, it was said, putting a defendant to trial without a lawyer would be "offensive to the common and fundamental ideas of fairness and right."[113] So justice at times played a role in the workings of our federalism. Why not in all criminal cases? How could a layman, even in a non-capital case, pick a jury? How could he use intelligently his peremptory challenges? How could he examine on the *voir dire* for cause? How could he build the case showing systematic exclusion of his race from the jury lists? How could it be that in a civilized country the Tenth Amendment allowed the States to follow such barbarous traditions? How could it ever be said that states' rights included the right to deny the poor a fair hearing, while according the full panoply of Due Process to the rich?

Over the years, however, most victories involving the rights of man have been won at the polls or in conventions of the people or in petitions such as produced the Magna Carta. But in recent decades a lethargy has possessed America. Those forces that once were a corrective influence are in the eclipse. The days of great public debate seem to have passed except on minor matters. The society of the dialogue has been vastly transformed as political processes have polarized at the center and to the right. Berlin, Laos, atomic testing and disarmament are hardly debated. A host of issues more vital in terms of survival than the Missouri Compromise, the *Dred Scott* decision, and the opinions that struck down Roosevelt's programs, go almost unnoticed when in early years they would have occupied the Senate for weeks on end. We are more and more informed by world-wide press coverage; yet we have lost some of our spirit of inquiry and challenge. We walk more and more in unison as if some mysterious force was herding us, a free people, in the manner in which the people of Russia and China are herded. The same docile attitude seems to have possessed most colleges and universities, most of the foundations, most of the press. Now that government has largely defaulted, where are the private groups who will marshal public opinion and gradually help us reclaim the ground lost and get legislative, if not constitutional, remedies for new oppressive practices that appear?

How can we expect to dishonor the non-conformist at home and still recognize his preeminence abroad? Overseas the voices heard are those of the unorthodox—those with queer sounding slogans and a socialist philosophy, those inclined to look with disdain and mistrust on the conservatism of our political thinking. Yet it is with these dissenters, with these off-beat leaders, that we must work if the ideological struggle is to be won. These non-conformists who shake the foundations of the feudal societies that make up most of the world seem to frighten us. We helped liquidate Mossadegh, the man who gave the villages of Persia their first vision of democracy. We helped set Thailand back 400 years in its political development. We have not been conspicuous overseas for our promotion of the Free Society in any area. The voice of dissent abroad by the time it reaches us is commonly called "communistic." But as Barbara Ward has said:

. . . the Communists did not create the desires and tensions of the emergent peoples. Modern industry and technology drew them into the web of world trade and set their feet on the first rung of the ladder of a modern economy. Communists or no Communists, they would try to climb the rest of the way.[114]

We overrate the Communists by attributing the world's discontent to them. They are well-organized. But they are overall minor, because the revolutions of the world relate not to communism but to disease, hunger, and lack of the decencies of life.

These revolutions would be underway even if the Communists suddenly evaporated. They are headed in each nation by leftists who want to get rid of feudalism and substitute the Free Society instead. We have little affinity for them. We seem to have a special affinity for war lords, dictators, and rulers of feudal regimes. Yet if we want to get on with the ideological contest, we must make the non-conformists in Asia, the Middle East, and Africa our intellectual allies.

The American experiment has much to offer the new nations. Legislative power, like executive power and judicial power, needs restraints. While custom and habit can supply those restraints, it takes centuries of experience to do so. The dilution of power by its diffusion and by precise delineation of the way in which it can be exercised is the essence of the American experiment. Few skilled in our system of government had any part to play in drafting the constitutions of the newly emerged nations. That was one price we paid for our preoccupation with military and financial foreign aid. We filled many underdeveloped nations with tanks and tractors. But at no time did we put in their libraries in a language they could read a two- or three-foot shelf of books that would supply guides to the creation of a Free Society and to an understanding of the service rendered by a Bill of Rights.

At no time did we indoctrinate our overseas personnel with the requirements of our Bill of Rights or with its history and service in making one community out of diverse elements. Our representatives abroad take their overseas posts fully apprised of the virtues of the free enterprise system and the American market system. But bills of attainder, ex post facto laws, habeas corpus, the Fifth Amendment, freedom of expression, separation of church and state—these are seldom conversation pieces in our embassies and legations. Yet it is around those subjects and allied constitutional topics that the fundamental differences between the Free Society and dictatorships (to the left and to the right) are to be found.

153

We conduct the ideological contest with ceaseless energy. But we disseminate more propaganda about our assumed virtues and achievements than knowledge about practical affairs that will help underdeveloped nations seek their salvation in the Free Society. Indeed many of our contestants—though able and loyal—are not trained for the contest. We have thought of the contest in terms of arms and guns, of the free enterprise and the American market system, when in truth it is a contest over checks and balances, separation of powers, freedom of speech, press, and religion, and freedom from the ever-present police. Concepts of freedom and equality can be infused into another culture only by earnest advocacy and vivid, practical illustrations of the need for protection of minorities against majority rule and for a diffusion of power among several groups so that none is supreme.

The relation of a community to its minorities is not peculiarly an American problem. Racial tensions characterize most communities the world over. The Communists erect a facade called "brotherhood." But in Russia—a nation of many races—the White Russian is preferred. In states like Kazakhistan, where the people are Mongol, the Russian gets 130 percent of the salary of the Kazakh who has the same skills and does the same work. The word "Jew" is stamped on every passport or identification paper. The segregated school system in Soviet Central Asia is one mark of racial prejudice.

No people experience discrimination more than the overseas Chinese in Southeast Asia. Koreans, under Japanese rule, could get no higher than file clerks. In Norway the Lapp is a second-class citizen. In Panama the Negro is kept out of the class of the entrepreneurs through a discriminatory licensing system. The Australians, whose standard of civil rights today is as high as any in the world, not so long ago hunted down the Aborigines in Tasmania until they succeeded in exterminating all of them—an experience supporting the thesis of the late A. Powell Davies that "History records no instance, so far as I am aware, of two or more races inhabiting the same territory for a considerable length of time without the race problem being ultimately solved either through absorption or extermination."[115]

We Americans seem to assume that all of us are born with knowledge of the Bill of Rights and with an insight into its mysteries. Most school boards, however, could not pass an examination on it. Neither could most parent-teacher associations. Teachers of government, like teachers of constitutional law, probably could. But most of our other teachers would fail. Yet knowledge of man's rights against government, the restraints on police, the place of the church in society should be known to all youth counsellors, if the oncoming generation is to be raised with a knowledge of the Free Society.

We have assumed that everyone will acquire this basic knowledge by an osmosis that comes from living here. Yet one has only to read the press to realize how remote from basic constitutional issues the editors are. They sound an alarm when a non-conformist is loose on a campus; they administer a sedative when a crime is "solved" by use of the third-degree method or a man is imprisoned for his beliefs. Only rarely do they give enlightenment, even in these days when the issues are drawn between the values of the Free Society and the dangers of a Communist regime. One has only to read the press and listen to public conversations to realize that few community leaders have ever been briefed on the Bill of Rights.

The task of any constitutional convention called today would be to increase, rather than merely restore, the original restraints placed on government. Some think that even the original Bill of Rights—particularly the Fifth Amendment—would not be adopted today. I think it would be, if the people gave a second, sober reflection to the problem. But if the Bill of Rights is to be restored in full vigor by the amending process and if additional restraints on government are to be fashioned, an intensive educational program is necessary. Even the watered-down version of the Bill of Rights we have today is not a sufficiently living force. Those who occupy the pulpits, those who write the editorials, teachers, as well as the school boards and parent-teachers associations, need re-education in the fundamentals. How is the community to be awakened? How are regimes of tolerance to be reinstated? How is the sense of wrath at the presence of injustice to be created?

Those interested in the world of computing machines often hold out hope that machines can in time relieve courts now bogged down with overwork. The facts in litigation are the most elusive elements in human conduct. That they may be found by push-button techniques is not worthy of serious consideration. One need not be a fact-skeptic of the stature of the late Jerome Frank to know that imponderables usually dominate the trial. We need not be profound students of history to know that words of the Constitution gain meaning and content from the value-judgments one puts into them. One who prefers the parliamentary system of government, as some judges do, will read Due Process one way. Those who take the system of checks and balances more seriously and read the Bill of Rights more literally find the guarantees to the individual more precise and the limitations on government more severe. These value-judgments are not those for robots. This is the controversy that must reach the precincts if the Bill of Rights is to be a continuous leavening influence.

No one way will be enough. Yet a good start can be made with the lawyers if we adopt the system of "law internships" that introduces the student to the problems of the poor who fill the magistrates' courts. The project that New York University School of Law has launched illustrates the potential of the "law internship" in the courts where law touches the lives of the people.

This project concerns bail. The handling of bail, especially in many of the larger cities of the United States, raises serious questions. The presumption that a man is innocent until proven guilty is in effect circumvented if a man is imprisoned, pending trial, because he cannot raise bail. The guarantee that bail will not be "excessive" presupposes the availability of bail.[116]

Apart from those heinous offenses against which society needs protection, bail should be set in light of the probability of the defendant's coming back for trial, or the probability of his remaining in the neighborhood.[117] For the indigent defendant, the problems can be most serious as he is unlikely to have the security which the bondsman demands. Not only does he lose his freedom, he loses the opportunity to investigate his case, to consult with his counsel (if any) outside the jail, and to earn money he may need to press his case.

Release of an indigent defendant on his own recognizance equalizes the position of the rich and the poor. The New York City Bail Project, in which students and faculty members of the New York University School of Law have participated, is an attempt to facilitate this solution.[118] Of the 150 defendants released on their own recognizance as of June, 1962, all but one had appeared for trial.

This system not only gives indigents equal protection of the law; it gives law students practical training in the application of the Bill of Rights. It indeed suggests that the "law internship" at the level of the magistrates' courts may be one way of producing a generation of lawyers whose vision of the law extends beyond the interests of those who offer the largest retainers.

The more tolerant of the unorthodox we are, the more respectful of minorities we become, the greater the chance of realizing the rich dividends of a Free Society. The greater our insistence on fair procedures by government, the greater the confidence in government. The more we encourage pluralistic tendencies at home, the greater our ability to manage the critical affairs of the world.

Can we expect people who live on the brink of a nuclear holocaust to be so bold and daring? I think so. Only the inventiveness that comes with a Free Society will produce the resourcefulness needed for survival, now that war is suicidal. Now that we face the problem of managing a world without war, we need a *consensus* with those we oppose on the ground rules that will *prevent* war and that will provide a rule of law for the settlement of disputes between nations.

To achieve these ends we need a renaissance in liberty at home. More regimentation, more dilution of the Bill of Rights means a lessening of our political ingenuity. The advantage of private enterprise over socialism is the manner in which it releases the energies, the imaginations, and the inventiveness of men. The advantage of fair procedures when the lone individual challenges those in power is that government becomes the symbol of justice, not the badge of oppression. The advantage of encouraging nonconformity is that new and fresh approaches to troublesome problems are encouraged. Once speech, belief, and conscience are placed beyond the reach of government, a nation acquires a spiritual strength that will make it a shining light to all who have never known the blessings of liberty, even to those behind the Iron and Bamboo Curtains.

NOTES

1. From the wealth of contemporary statements to this effect, I choose Dr. Benjamin Rush's because it was made in Philadelphia during the Constitutional Convention. In his July 4th oration, he said: "The American War is over; but this is far from being the case with the American Revolution. On the contrary, nothing but the first act of the great drama is closed. It remains yet to establish and perfect our new forms of Government; and to prepare the principles, morals and manners of our citizens for these forms of Government after they are established and brought to perfection." Warren, The Making of the Constitution 270 (1929). In the next generation, Rush's son, Richard, was one of those who continued the theme of America's essential newness. Miller, The Legal Mind in America from Independence to the Civil War (1962).

2. Letter from James Madison to Thomas Jefferson, Oct. 17, 1788.

3. 3 Elliot's Debates 561 (2d ed. 1836). Of course, the English Bill of Rights did contain some strong and categorical clauses, especially those dealing with the Protestant succession, but none that met the aspirations of a democratic republic.

4. 6 The Writings of James Madison 83 (Hunt ed. 1906).

5. Madison repeatedly emphasized England's lack of provision for the rights which Americans considered most important. E.g., in his address of June 8, 1789 submitting the Amendments to Congress, in

the articles he contributed to The National Gazette in 1792, and in his Report on the Virginia Resolutions in 1800.

6. Speech of June 8, 1789, 1 Annals of Cong. 457 (1834).

7. Pursuant to Swift v. Tyson, 41 U.S. (16 Pet.) 1 (1842).

8. Erie R.R. v. Tompkins, 304 U.S. 64 (1938).

9. See Weems v. United States, 217 U.S. 349 (1910).

10. Trop v. Dulles, 356 U.S. 86 (1958).

11. Robinson v. California, 370 U.S. 660 (1962). The California law nullified in this case reminds one embarrassingly of Samuel Butler's "Erewhon." It is almost a century since Butler travestied the penology of his day by picturing a society so morally obtuse that it made sickness a criminal offense.

12. Speech of June 8, 1789, 1 Annals of Cong. 449 (1834).

CHAPTER 2

1. Madison, Vices of the Political System of the United States, in 2 The Writings of James Madison 361, 364 (Hunt ed. 1901).

2. Madison, of Ancient & Modern Confederacies, in 2 The Writings of James Madison 369 (Hunt ed. 1901).

3. Letter From James Madison to Edmund Randolph, April 8, 1787, in id. at 336; Letter From James Madison to George Washington, April 16, 1787, in id. at 344.

4. Three variant texts of the Virginia Plan appear in Tansill, Documents Illustrative of the Formation of the Union 953–63 (1927).

5. 1 Annals of Cong. 424, 431–42 (1834).

6. Letter From James Madison to William Bradford, Jr., Jan. 24, 1774, in 1 The Writings of James Madison 18, 19 (Hunt ed. 1900).

7. Gwathmey, Twelve Virginia Counties 126 (1937).

8. Letter From James Madison to William Bradford, Jr., Jan. 24, 1774, in 1 The Writings of James Madison 18, 21 (Hunt ed. 1900).

9. Letter from James Madison to William Bradford, Jr., April 1, 1774, in id. at 22, 23–24.

10. Thomson, Notes: Summaries of Debates by the Secretary of Congress, in 6 Burnett, Letters of Members of the Continental Congress 481–88 (1933).

11. Madison, Memorial and Remonstrance Against Religious Assessments, in 2 The Writings of James Madison 183, 184–85 (Hunt ed. 1901).

12. Madison, Vices of the Political System of the United States, in id. at 361, 366.

13. Madison, Notes of the Debates in the Federal Convention of 1787, at 27 (session of May 30, 1787) (Hunt-Scott ed. 1920).

14. Id. at 24 (session of May 29, 1787). For strategic reasons, to bring Governor Randolph by degrees to a position he at first resisted, Madison omitted this resolve from the plan as Randolph submitted it to the convention. The Governor himself offered it after other delegates pointed out that the substitute, calling for enlargement of the Articles of Confederation, was in conflict with all that followed.

15. Id. at 353 (session of Aug. 7, 1787).

16. Id. at 619, 622 (app. VII n. 2).

17. The Library of Congress is custodian of the original manuscript, delivered April 1, 1837, by Mrs. Madison with other original manuscripts comprising The Madison Papers (1840). Madison marked out the word "grave" from his remark that he had doubts about the feasibility of an enumeration of powers, but retained the statement that his doubts were increasing. One of the additions from Yates heightened his nationalism.

18. The Federalist No. 10, at 59 (Lodge ed. 1891) (Madison).

19. The Federalist No. 39, at 233 (Lodge ed. 1891) (Madison).

20. The Federalist No. 57, at 356 (Lodge ed. 1891). In the light of modern scholarship, especially the researches of Edward Gaylord Bourne (Am. Hist. Rev., April 1897) and Douglass Adair (William and Mary Q., April, July 1944), I have pursued the same course that Charles A. Beard did in the Enduring Federalist (1948) and ascribed Nos. 49–58 to Madison without regard to the ancient dispute over their authorship.

21. The Federalist No. 44, at 282 (Lodge ed. 1891) (Madison). The Chief Justice's definition was: "Let the end be legitimate, let it be within the scope of the constitution, and all means which are appropriate, which are plainly adapted to that end, which are not prohibited, but consist with the letter and spirit of the constitution, are constitutional." McCulloch v. Maryland, 17 U.S. (4 Wheat.) 316, 421 (1819).

22. 2 Rives, History of the Life and Times of James Madison 612 (1866).

23. Letter From George Washington to Marquis de Lafayette, April 28, 1788, in 2 The Writings of George Washington 254, 256 (Ford ed. 1891).

24. Madison, Notes of the Debates in the Federal Convention of 1787 at 449–50 (session of Aug. 22, 1787) (Hunt-Scott ed. 1920).

25. Letter From James Madison to George Eve, Jan. 2, 1789, in 5 The Writings of James Madison 391 n.l, 320 (Hunt ed. 1904).

26. 1 Annals of Cong. 424, 431–42 (1834).

27. Id. at 435, 440–41. Although the protections thrown around accused persons in the fourth, fifth, sixth and eighth amendments are directed by implication toward federal courts, there is one of them that is not effective as a federal protection unless it applies also to the states. That is the provision, "nor shall any person be subject for the same offense to be twice put in jeopardy of life or limb." It is highly significant that the Annals of Congress for Aug. 17, 1789 (at which time the words were in different order) contain the following entry: "Mr. Partridge moved to insert, after 'same offense,' the words 'by any law of the United States.' This amendment was lost also." The only conceivable reason for this motion by the Massachusetts representative was to exclude state courts from the prohibition. Since the effect of it in creating double jeopardy must have been understood, its defeat creates a presumption that full protection was intended. That is suggested also by approval in debate of the British rule that acquittal is final even if conclusive proof of guilt appears afterwards.

28. 1 Annals of Cong. at 441 (1934).

29. Id. at 439.

30. 3 Annals of Cong. 899 (1834).

31. Id. at 934. He wrote in the same vein to Monroe a week later. Letter From James Madison to James Monroe, Dec. 4, 1794, in 6 The Writings of James Madison 219, 221–24 (Hunt ed. 1906).

32. 71 U.S. (4 Wall.) 277 (1866).

33. Letter From Mathew Carey to James Madison, Oct. 30, 1814, in Papers of James Madison, Library of Congress.

34. Washington National Intelligencer, March 10, 1817.

CHAPTER 3

1. See also ch. II supra, Brant, The Madison Heritage.

2. 32 U.S. (7 Pet.) 242, 249 (1833).

3. 332 U.S. 46, 71–72 (1947) (dissenting opinion).

4. 361 U.S. 147, 155 (1959) (concurring opinion).

5. See The Trial of John Liburne and John Wharton (Star Chamber 1637) in 3 How. St. Tr. 1315 (1816).

6. Leveller Manifestoes of the Puritan Revolution 423 (Wolfe ed. 1944).

7. 1 Rives, History of the Life and Times of James Madison 44 (1859).

8. 4 Jefferson, Writings 506 (Washington ed. 1859).

9. 5 U.S. (1 Cranch) 137 (1803).

10. 1 Annals of Cong. 437 (1834).

11. Ibid.

12. 1 Annals of Cong. 434 (1834).

13. 1 Annals of Cong. 738 (1834).
14. 6 The Writings of James Madison 391 (Hunt ed. 1906).
15. 5 The Writings of James Madison 176 (Hunt ed. 1904).
16. Id. at 132.
17. 1 Annals of Cong. 730 (1834). (Emphasis added.)
18. 1 Annals of Cong. 436 (1834).
19. See Joint Anti-Fascist Refugee Comm. v. McGrath, 341 U.S. 123, 146–49 (1951) (appendix to concurring opinion of Black, J.).
20. 1 Annals of Cong. 437 (1834).
21. 1 Annals of Cong. 439 (1834).
22. 8 Jefferson, Writings 2–3 (Washington ed. 1859).

CHAPTER 4

1. The Federalist No. 45, at 290 (Lodge ed. 1891).
2. Adams, The Jubilee of the Constitution 115 (1839).
3. Texas v. White, 74 U.S. (7 Wall.) 700, 725 (1868).
4. 1 Annals of Cong. 439 (1834).
5. See Dumbauld, The Bill of Rights and What It Means Today 215 (1957).
6. 1 Annals of Cong. 440 (1834).
7. Ibid.
8. Id. at 755.
9. Rawle, A View of the Constitution of the United States of America 120–21 (1825).
10. 32 U.S. (7 Pet.) 243 (1833).
11. Id. at 246.
12. Id. at 247.
13. See, e.g., Lessee of Livingston v. Moore, 32 U.S. (7 Pet.) 469, 551–52 (1833); Permoli v. Municipality No. 1, 44 U.S. (3 How.) 589, 609 (1845) (dictum); Fox v. Ohio, 46 U.S. (5 How.) 410, 434–35 (1847); Smith v. Maryland, 59 U.S. (18 How.) 71, 76 (1855); Withers v. Buckley, 61 U.S. (20 How.) 84, 89–91 (1857).
14. 1 Annals of Cong. 436 (1834).
15. Fairman, Does the Fourteenth Amendment Incorporate the Bill of Rights?—The Original Understanding, 2 Stan. L. Rev. 5, 9 (1949).
16. Public Letter by Orville H. Browning, Oct. 13, 1866, Cincinnati Commercial, Oct. 26, 1866, p. 2, col. 4, quoted in Fairman, supra note 15, at 78.
17. Fairman, supra note 15, at 21.
18. 83 U.S. (16 Wall.) 36 (1872).
19. Twining v. New Jersey, 211 U.S. 78, 96 (1908).
20. 83 U.S. (16 Wall.) at 77–78.

21. See Walker v. Sauvinet, 92 U.S. 90 (1875); United States v. Cruikshank, 92 U.S. 542, 552–56 (1875); Hurtado v. California, 110 U.S. 516 (1884); Presser v. Illinois, 116 U.S. 252, 263–68 (1886).

22. In re Kemmler, 136 U.S. 436, 448 (1890); McElvaine v. Brush, 142 U.S. 155, 158–59 (1891); O'Neil v. Vermont, 144 U.S. 323, 332 (1892) (dictum); Maxwell v. Dow, 176 U.S. 581, 597–98 (1900); Twining v. New Jersey, 211 U.S. 78, 96 (1908). See Spies v. Illinois, 123 U.S. 131 (1887). See generally Morrison, Does the Fourteenth Amendment Incorporate the Bill of Rights?—The Judicial Interpretation, 2 Stan. L. Rev. 140 (1949).

23. O'Neil v. Vermont, supra note 22, at 363, 370 (dissenting opinions).

24. 332 U.S. 46, 68 (1947). For contrasting views of the incorporation of the first eight amendments by the Fourteenth Amendment, compare Flack, The Adoption of the Fourteenth Amendment (1908), with Fairman, supra note 15.

25. 332 U.S. at 71–72.

26. Mr. Justice Douglas joined in Mr. Justice Black's opinion. Mr. Justice Murphy stated that he and Mr. Justice Rutledge would go further: "I agree that the specific guarantees of the Bill of Rights should be carried over intact into the first section of the Fourteenth Amendment. But I am not prepared to say that the latter is entirely and necessarily limited by the Bill of Rights. Occasions may arise where a proceeding falls so far short of conforming to fundamental standards of procedure as to warrant constitutional condemnation in terms of a lack of due process despite the absence of a specific provision in the Bill of Rights." Id. at 124.

27. Twining v. New Jersey, 211 U.S. 78, 99 (1908).

28. Adamson v. California, 332 U.S. 46, 66 (1947) (concurring opinion).

29. Palko v. Connecticut, 302 U.S. 319, 326 (1937). (Emphasis added.)

30. Twining v. New Jersey, 211 U.S. 78, 99–100 (1908).

31. Id. at 106.

32. Palko v. Connecticut, 302 U.S. 319, 325 (1937).

33. Hurtado v. California, 110 U.S. 516, 535 (1884).

34. Snyder v. Massachusetts, 291 U.S. 97, 105 (1934).

35. 259 U.S. 530, 543 (1922).

36. See West Virginia State Bd. of Educ. v. Barnette, 319 U.S. 624, 633 (1943); Bridges v. California, 314 U.S. 252, 277 (1941); Cantwell v. Connecticut, 310 U.S. 296, 303 (1940); De Jonge v. Oregon, 299 U.S. 353, 364 (1937); Near v. Minnesota ex rel. Olson, 283 U.S. 697, 707 (1931); Gitlow v. New York, 268 U.S. 652, 666 (1925). See generally Dumbauld, supra note 5, at 133–34.

37. Palko v. Connecticut, 302 U.S. 319, 327 (1937).
38. See Smith v. California, 361 U.S. 147, 169 (1959) (separate opinion by Mr. Justice Harlan); Roth v. United States, 354 U.S. 476. 505–06 (1957) (separate opinion by Mr. Justice Harlan); Beauharnais v. Illinois, 343 U.S. 250, 288 (1952) (dissenting opinion by Mr. Justice Jackson).
39. 1 Annals of Cong. 439 (1834).
40. See Black, Ch. III.
41. 1 Annals of Cong. 437 (1834).
42. Chicago, B. & Q.R.R. v. Chicago, 166 U.S. 226, 241 (1897).
43. Powell v. Alabama, 287 U.S. 45, 68–69 (1932).
44. Weeks v. United States, 232 U.S. 383, 398 (1914).
45. Wolf v. Colorado, 338 U.S. 25, 27–28 (1949).
46. Hebert v. Louisiana, 272 U.S. 312, 316 (1926).
47. Walker v. Sauvinet, 92 U.S. 90 (1875).
48. E.g., Palko v. Connecticut, 302 U.S. 319, 324 (1937).
49. 1 Annals of Cong. 437 (1834).
50. Betts v. Brady, 316 U.S. 455 (1942).
51. McNeal v. Culver, 365 U.S. 109, 111 (1961), quoting Uveges v. Pennsylvania, 335 U.S. 437, 441 (1948).
52. Id. at 117 (concurring opinion).
53. Rawle, supra note 9, at 127–28.
54. McNeal v. Culver, 365 U.S. 109, 118 (1961) (concurring opinion).
55. Griffin v. Illinois, 351 U.S. 12 (1956).
56. Spano v. New York, 360 U.S. 315, 320–31 (1959).
57. See, e.g., Elkins v. United States, 364 U.S. 206 (1960); Mallory v. United States, 354 U.S. 449 (1957); McNabb v. United States, 318 U.S. 332 (1943).
58. E.g., mob domination of a trial: Moore v. Dempsey, 261 U.S. 86 (1923); the right to counsel: Powell v. Alabama, 287 U.S. 45 (1932); the effect of perjured testimony: Mooney v. Holohan, 294 U.S. 103 (1935); Alcorta v. Texas, 335 U.S. 28 (1957) (per curiam); coerced confessions: Brown v. Mississippi, 297 U.S. 278 (1936); double jeopardy: Palko v. Connecticut, 302 U.S. 319 (1937); Hoag v. New Jersey, 356 U.S. 464 (1958); Ciucci v. Illinois, 356 U.S. 571 (1958) (per curiam).
59. Weeks v. United States, 232 U.S. 383, 398 (1914).
60. Wolf v. Colorado, 338 U.S. 25 (1949).
61. Elkins v. United States, 364 U.S. 206 (1960).
62. Wolf v. Colorado, 338 U.S. 25, 40, 41, 47 (1949) (dissenting opinions of Justices Douglas, Murphy and Rutledge).
63. Cardozo, The Nature of the Judicial Process 84 (1921).

64. Schaefer, Federalism and State Criminal Procedure, 70 Harv. L. Rev. 1, 26 (1956).
65. Ohio ex rel. Eaton v. Price, 364 U.S. 263, 275 (1960) (dissenting from the judgment of an equally divided Court).
66. See, e.g., People v. DenUyl, 318 Mich. 645, 651, 29 N.W.2d 284, 287 (1947), in which the Supreme Court of Michigan applied the state privilege against self-incrimination to exonerate from disclosure whenever there is a probability of prosecution in state or federal jurisdictions. "It seems like a travesty on verity to say that one is not subjected to self-incrimination when compelled to give testimony in a State judicial proceeding which testimony may forthwith be used against him in a Federal criminal prosecution." But see, as to the federal privilege under the Fifth Amendment, United States v. Murdock, 284 U.S. 141 (1931).

See also Tex. Code Crim. Proc. art. 494 (Supp. 1960): "Whenever it is made known to the court at an arraignment or any other time that an accused charged with a felony is too poor to employ a counsel, the court shall appoint one (1) or more practicing attorneys to defend him."

And see proposed Ark. H.B. 111, introduced January 17, 1961. The conviction or acquittal of an offense against the United States, under this bill, would constitute a bar to Arkansas prosecution for the same offense. Cf. Bartkus v. Illinois, 359 U.S. 121 (1959), which itself has been overruled by an Illinois statute, Ill. Ann. Stat. ch. 38, § 601.1 (Smith-Hurd Supp. 1960), passed shortly after the Court's decision. This statute provides, "Whenever on the trial of an accused person for the violation of any criminal law of this State it is shown that he has previously been tried and convicted or acquitted under the laws of the Federal government, which former trial was based on the act or omission for which he is being tried in this State, it is a sufficient defense."

67. See Douglas, Vagrancy and Arrest on Suspicion, 70 Yale L.J. 1 (1960).
68. 1 Annals of Cong. 432 (1834).

CHAPTER 5

1. Ch. III, Black, The Bill of Rights and the Federal Government.
2. Ch. IV, Brennan, The Bill of Rights and the States.
3. 5 Freeman, George Washington 477 (1952).
4. 3 Channing, A History of the United States 376 (1912).
5. 24 Writings of Washington 272 (Fitzpatrick ed. 1938).
6. The Federalist No. 41, at 251 (Lodge ed. 1888) (Madison).
7. See, e.g., Pinkney's recommendations to the Federal Conven-

tion, 2 Records of the Federal Convention 341 (Farrand ed. 1911), and the discussion by Mason and Madison, id. at 617; Resolutions on Ratification of the Constitution by the States of Massachusetts, New Hampshire, New York and Virginia, reprinted in Documents Illustrative of Formation of the Union of American States, H.R. Doc. No. 398, 69th Cong., 1st Sess. 1018–20, 1024–44 (1927).

8. The vote in the House was for: 220, against: 105, not voting: 104. In the Senate the vote was for: 47, against: 21, not voting: 28. 96 Cong. Rec. 14931, 14973 (1950).

9. See, e.g., Remarks of Representatives Wolverton and Hoffman and Senators Watkins and Cain, 96 Cong. Rec. 14835, 14919, 15177, A6561 (1950).

10. 68 U.S. (1 Wall.) 243 (1863).

11. 61 U.S. (20 How.) 65 (1857).

12. Report of Secretary of War Knox to the Congress on the Military Force in 1789, communicated to the Senate on August 10, 1789, 1 American State Papers—Military Affairs No. 1. At the time of the Constitutional Conventions, consideration was given to limiting the size of the National Army for all time to a few thousand men, through express constitutional provision. 2 Records of the Federal Convention 323, 329, 330, 616–17 (Farrand ed. 1911).

13. Total strength of the armed forces on November 30, 1961, was estimated to be 2,780,975 by the Directorate of Statistical Services, Office of the Secretary of Defense, Pamphlet 22.1 (Dec. 20, 1961).

14. The Universal Military Training and Service Act of 1951, §§ 4(b), (d), establishes an active duty tour of two years and a reserve obligation of six years thereafter, as the norm for all persons subject to the Act. 65 Stat. 78 (1951), as amended, 50 U.S.C. App. §§ 454(b), (d) (1958). In statistics compiled in 1959, the American male between 20 and 25 had a life expectancy of another 49.5 years. Nat'l Office of Vital Statistics, Life Tables § 5–5 (Dep't of Health, Educ. & Welfare 1959).

15. On June 30, 1960, the Veterans Administration counted 22,534,000 veterans of all armed forces then living. 1960 Adm'r of Veterans Affairs Ann. Rep. 6–7 (1961).

16. 346 U.S. 137 (1953).

17. See Uniform Code of Military Justice, 10 U.S.C. §§ 867, 876 (1958).

18. Similarly, since the adoption of the Uniform Code of Military Justice, the Court of Claims has not granted relief in the form of back pay to claimants alleging wrongful dismissal from government service through court martial proceedings lacking fundamental fairness. Compare Shapiro v. United States, 69 F. Supp. 205 (Ct. Cl. 1947).

19. Quinn, The United States Court of Military Appeals and Military Due Process, 35 St. John's L. Rev. 225, 232 (1961). In an early opinion, the Court of Military Appeals said, "If, because of the peculiarities of the military service, a variation from civilian practice is necessary to assure a fair trial, we should unhesitatingly adopt the procedure best suited to the administration of military justice, even though by so doing we may bring about a departure from a prior service rule." United States v. Hemp, 1 U.S.C.M.A. 280, 286, 3 C.M.R. 14, 20 (1952). Compare the evolution of the court's approach to "military due process" in United States v. Clay, 1 U.S.C.M.A. 74, 1 C.M.R. 74 (1951), with United States v. Jacoby, 11 U.S.C.M.A. 428, 29 C.M.R. 244 (1960).

20. United States v. Jacoby, supra note 19, at 430–31, 29 C.M.R. at 246–47.

21. Dep't of the Army Pamphlet No. 27–101–18 (Oct. 7, 1959), reprinted in 1960 U.S.C.M.A. Ann. Rep. 4. Similar views have been expressed by ranking officers of the Army and Navy. See Army Chief of Staff General Decker, id., and Navy Judge Advocate General Admiral Mott, An Appraisal of Proposed Changes in the Uniform Code of Military Justice, 35 St. John's L. Rev. 300 (1961).

22. Wilson v. Girard, 354 U.S. 524 (1957).

23. The Schooner Exchange v. McFaddon, 11 U.S. (7 Cranch) 116 (1812).

24. A recent survey by the Department of Defense lists 19 countries with which the United States has entered Status of Forces Agreements similar to the one with which the Court dealt in Girard. In addition, this country is signatory to agreements with 56 nations (15 the same as SOFA signatories) in which military missions (as distinguished from troop deployments) have virtual diplomatic immunity. See also U.S. Dep't of State, Treaties in Force (Jan. 1, 1962).

25. See Senate Comm. on Armed Services, Operation of Article VII, NATO Status of Forces Treaty, S. Rep. No. 1041, 87th Cong., 1st Sess. 2 (1961).

26. 356 U.S. 86 (1958).

27. 71 U.S. (4 Wall.) 2 (1866).

28. Id. at 119.

29. In times of stress, the Court is not only vulnerable, to some extent, to the emotions of our people, but also to action by Congress in restricting what that body may consider judicial interference with the needs of security and defense. Following the Civil War, Congress actually exercised its constitutional powers to provide for the rules governing the appellate jurisdiction of the Supreme Court, for this very purpose. See Ex parte McCardle, 73 U.S. (6 Wall.) 318 (1867); 74 U.S. (7 Wall.) 506 (1868).

30. 320 U.S. 81 (1943).
31. 323 U.S. 214 (1944).
32. Chief Justice Hughes, speaking for the Court in Home Bldg. & Loan Ass'n v. Blaisdell, 290 U.S. 398, 426 (1934).
33. In this connection, we might also consider and compare the cases of Ex parte Quirin, 317 U.S. 1 (1942), and Abel v. United States, 362 U.S. 217 (1960). The former came before the Court at the outset of World War II, at a time when the outlook for the survival of the free world was dim. On the floor of Congress, fears were expressed that Hitler could subdue the country even without an invasion, through the use of "fifth columnists" and German allies thought to exist in every State of the Union. See 87 Cong. Rec. 555 (1941). When a small group of Nazi saboteurs was discovered on our shores, they were brought before a military tribunal—not our civilian courts. They were treated as wartime belligerents and spies, and ordered executed. The Supreme Court denied an application for a writ of habeas corpus, sustaining the military's jurisdiction.

However, when, in June 1957, Rudolph Abel was apprehended in his New York hotel room and identified as a Colonel in the Russian army, he was not brought before a court martial. A full civilian trial, with all the safeguards of our Bill of Rights, was accorded this agent of our adversary. Abel brought his case to the Supreme Court claiming the protection of our Constitution. I was among those who dissented from the Court's judgment that he had not been the subject of a constitutionally proscribed search and seizure. But all of the opinions reiterated our fundamental approach—that neither the nature of the case nor the notoriety of the defendant could influence our decision on the constitutional issue presented.

Cf. In re Yamashita, 327 U.S. 1 (1946), in which the Court denied habeas corpus relief to an officer of the enemy vanquished in a war fought in the cause of the Constitution, but who, for his wartime actions, was subjected to an American military court whose procedures were questionably squared with the spirit of due process.
34. 354 U.S. 1 (1957), withdrawing 351 U.S. 487 (1956).
35. McElroy v. United States ex rel. Guagliardo, 361 U.S. 281 (1960) (employee—noncapital offense); Grisham v. Hagan, 361 U.S. 278 (1960) (employee—capital offense); Kinsella v. United States ex rel. Singleton, 361 U.S. 234 (1960) (dependent—noncapital offense).
36. Brief for Petitioner, the Secretary of Defense, pp. 12, 71, 110–11, McElroy v. United States ex rel. Guagliardo, 361 U.S. 281 (1960).
37. United States ex rel. Toth v. Quarles, 350 U.S. 11 (1955).

38. Id. at 22.
39. 355 U.S. 579 (1958).
40. 327 U.S. 304 (1946). Cf. Madsen v. Kinsella, 343 U.S. 341 (1952).
41. For example, in Bell v. United States, 366 U.S. 393 (1961), the Army was challenged for declining to pay former soldiers who, during the Korean War, and while prisoners of war of the enemy, had betrayed some fellow prisoners and had refused initial opportunities for repatriation. Despite the absence of any authority for withholding the pay earned and accrued by these men to the dates of their well-deserved dishonorable discharges, the Army refused to make payment. As the situation was summarized by the dissenting judge in the Court of Claims, "Finding nothing in the law books to justify its refusal to pay these men, it threw the books away and just refused to pay them. It could have set before these confused young men a better example of government by law." 181 F. Supp. 668, 675 (Ct. Cl. 1960). We agreed.

In similar vein have been the series of decisions concerning the conscription procedures of the Selective Service System. For example, this Term we have again had occasion to consider a conviction based on an alleged failure of a registrant to notify his draft board of a change of address. After three unsuccessful prosecutions for draft evasion, the Government secured a belated indictment, conviction and three-year prison sentence for the young man's questionable failure to notify his board promptly of a change of address. But, from the record, it seemed clear that it was the registrant's annoying persistence in pursuing appellate rights to secure an exemption from active duty on a claim of being a minister of Jehovah's Witnesses, that underlay the course of prosecution. Venus v. United States, 368 U.S. 345 (1961) (mem.). In 1955, in Gonzales v. United States, 348 U.S. 407 (1955), we were faced with a conviction for draft evasion, in which the draftee had not been accorded the simple right of examining a Department of Justice memorandum contesting his claims that he was a conscientious objector, and which memorandum had been presented to a Selective Service appeal board in reviewing Gonzales' classification. Understandably, we held that although the needs of the Army were great, it had to be fair in abiding by the law under which it sought conscripts. An additional factor of importance about these cases is that under the Selective Service law, violation of the call to military duty is a civil offense, punishable only in the civilian courts.

42. The Defense Department now spends over 50% of the total federal budget, a sum almost 10% of our gross national product. It is estimated that 10% of the entire national labor force is, in some

NOTES TO PAGES 107 TO 113

manner, employed in defense industries or the defense establishment itself. See N.Y. Times, May 21, 1961, p. 48, cols. 4–5; U.S. Dept. of Commerce, Statistical Abstract of the United States 235, 301 (1961).

43. 343 U.S. 579 (1952).

44. Id. at 634–35.

45. 361 U.S. 39 (1959).

46. 10 Complete Works of Abraham Lincoln 66 (Nicolay and Hay ed. 1894).

47. 360 U.S. 474 (1959).

48. 367 U.S. 886 (1961).

49. For decisions in a comparable vein, see Cole v. Young, 351 U.S. 536 (1956), limiting, through interpretation to those in "sensitive" positions, the power of the Executive summarily to dismiss government employees in the interest of "national security"; Vitarelli v. Seaton, 359 U.S. 535 (1959), requiring government agencies dismissing employees in nonsensitive positions on security grounds, to afford the employees an opportunity to see the charges against them and to confront adverse witnesses; Kent v. Dulles, 357 U.S. 116 (1958), upholding the right of citizens to travel freely in the absence of compelling restrictions clearly to be found in Congressional action.

50. See, e.g., McKinney v. Missouri-K.-T.R.R., 357 U.S. 265 (1958); Hyland v. Watson, 287 F.2d 884 (6th Cir.), cert. denied, 368 U.S. 876 (1961). Cf. the recent decision of Australia's highest court invalidating a far reaching veteran's preference statute on the ground that with the World War II emergency past, the war power justification for such laws, under the Australian Constitution, had ceased. Illawarra District County Council v. Wickham, 101 Commw. L.R. 467 (Austl. 1959).

51. N.Y. Times, Jan. 18, 1961, p. 22, cols. 5, 6.

52. President Kennedy, in his special message to Congress on the defense budget delivered shortly after taking office, declared, "Neither our strategy nor our psychology as a nation—and certainly not our economy—must become dependent upon our . . . maintenance of a large military establishment. . . . Our arms must be subject to ultimate civilian control and command at all times . . ." N.Y. Times, March 29, 1961, p. 16, cols. 1, 2.

Similarly, President Truman, on such occasions as his message to Congress urging the creation of a single Department of Defense, over which a civilian would preside, and his removal of General MacArthur as Commander of United Nations forces in Korea, reiterated these beliefs. 1945 Public Papers of the Presidents of the United States: Harry S. Truman 554–55, 558 (1961); 2 Truman, Memoirs 449 (1956).

CHAPTER 6

1. 1 De Tocqueville, Democracy in America 259 (Bradley ed. 1945).

2. 2 De Tocqueville, Democracy in America 110 (Bradley ed. 1945).

3. Frankfurter, Law and Politics 16 (1939).

4. Beinart, The South African Appeal Court and Judicial Review, 21 Modern L. Rev. 587, 593 (1958); Harris, The Constitutional Crisis in South Africa, 103 Sol. J. 995, 997 (1959).

5. Landis, South African Apartheid Legislation II: Extension, Enforcement and Perpetuation, 71 Yale L.J. 437 (1962).

6. Bagehot, The English Constitution 92 (2d ed. 1873).

7. 5 The Writings of James Madison 273 (Hunt ed. 1904).

8. The Federalist No. 48, at 347 (Wright ed. 1961) (Madison).

9. 5 The Writings of James Madison 274 (Hunt ed. 1904).

10. O'Meara v. State Bd. Against Discrimination, 58 Wash. 2d 793, 365 P. 2d 1 (1961).

11. Dash, The Eavesdroppers 68–69 (1959).

12. 2 De Tocqueville, Democracy in America 11–12 (Bradley ed. 1945).

13. See, e.g., Czechoslovak Law No. 140/1961 Coll. on Instigation, § 100(1), (2) (Jan. 1, 1962).

14. Minneapolis Star, Nov. 18, 1961, p. 6a, col. 1.

15. Lacy, Freedom and Communications 69 (1961).

16. Id. at 71.

17. 1 De Tocqueville, Democracy in America 186–87 (Bradley ed. 1945).

18. N. W. Ayre & Son, Directory of Newspapers and Periodicals 11 (1942); p. 7 (1952); p. xix (1962).

19. 3 Diary and Autobiography of John Adams 293 (Butterfield ed. 1961).

20. Frank v. Maryland, 359 U.S. 360 (1959).

21. Abel v. United States, 362 U.S. 217 (1960).

22. See Bandy v. United States, 81 Sup. Ct. 197 (1960); 82 Sup. Ct. 11 (1961).

23. 342 U.S. 524 (1952).

24. Dennis v. United States, 341 U.S. 494 (1951).

25. 367 U.S. 203 (1961).

26. Chafee, Free Speech in the United States 21 (1948).

27. Levy, The Legacy of Suppression 236–37 (1960).

28. See Meiklejohn, Book Review, 35 So. Cal. L. Rev. 111, 117 (1961).

29. 4 Elliot's Debates 528–29 (2d ed. 1836).

30. Betts v. Brady, 316 U.S. 455 (1942); Powell v. Alabama, 287 U.S. 45 (1932).
31. 110 U.S. 516, 541 (1884) (dissenting opinion).
32. 342 U.S. 165 (1952).
33. 352 U.S. 432 (1957).
34. Frankfurter, Law and Politics 13 (1939).
35. 10 U.S. (6 Cranch) 48, 77 (1810).
36. 14 Papers of Thomas Jefferson 661 (Boyd ed. 1958).
37. 28 U.S.C. § 2254 (1958).
38. Darr v. Burford, 339 U.S. 200 (1950).
39. United States v. Carver, 260 U.S. 482, 490 (1923).
40. Mattox v. Sacks, 369 U.S. 656 (1962).
41. 344 U.S. 443, 482 (1953).
42. Id. at 485–86.
43. Id. at 557 (dissenting opinion).
44. Meredith v. Winter Haven, 320 U.S. 228 (1943).
45. See, e.g., Harrison v. NAACP, 360 U.S. 167, 176–78 (1959).
46. See, e.g., United Gas Pipe Line Co. v. Ideal Cement Co., 369 U.S. 134 (1962) (per curiam).
47. 333 U.S. 103 (1948).
48. 223 U.S. 118 (1912).
49. 48 U.S. (7 How.) 1 (1849).
50. 287 U.S. 378 (1932).
51. 2 Ld. Raym. 938, 956, 92 Eng. Rep. 126, 138 (K.B. 1702).
52. 73 U.S. (6 Wall.) 50 (1867).
53. Sterling v. Constantin, 287 U.S. 378 (1932).
54. Hirabayashi v. United States, 320 U.S. 81 (1943); Korematsu v. United States, 319 U.S. 432 (1943).
55. See United States v. Smith, 286 U.S. 6, 33 (1932).
56. 369 U.S. 186 (1962).
57. Aetna Life Ins. Co. v. Haworth, 300 U.S. 227 (1937).
58. United Public Workers v. Mitchell, 330 U.S. 75, 89 (1947).
59. 4 Holdsworth, A History of English Law 355 (1924).
60. See United States ex rel. Marcus v. Hess, 317 U.S. 537, 542 (1943).
61. Administrative Procedure Act § 10(a), 60 Stat. 243 (1946), 5 U.S.C. § 1009(a) (1958).
62. H.R. Doc. No. 986, 76th Cong., 3d Sess. 2, 3, 11 (1940).
63. L. Singer & Sons v. Union Pac. R.R., 311 U.S. 295, 304 (1940); FCC v. Sanders Bros. Radio Station, 309 U.S. 470, 477 (1940).
64. Associated Industries, Inc. v. Ickes, 134 F.2d 694, 704 (1943).
65. City of Atlanta v. Ickes, 308 U.S. 517 (1939) (per curiam).
66. Tennessee Elec. Power Co. v. TVA, 306 U.S. 118 (1939).

67. Poe v. Ullman, 367 U.S. 497 (1961).
68. Frothingham v. Mellon, 262 U.S. 447, 486 (1923).
69. Id. at 487.
70. Ibid.
71. 342 U.S. 429 (1952).
72. Id. at 434.
73. 330 U.S. 1 (1947).
74. See Buchanan v. Warley, 245 U.S. 60, 72–73 (1917); Mitchell v. United States, 313 U.S. 80 (1941); Evers v. Dwyer, 358 U.S. 202 (1958).
75. 239 U.S. 33, 38–39 (1915).
76. Note, The Void-For-Vagueness Doctrine in the Supreme Court, 109 U. Pa. L. Rev. 67, 75 (1960).
77. Herndon v. Lowry, 301 U.S. 242, 264 (1937). See also Winters v. New York, 333 U.S. 507 (1948).
78. Kent v. Dulles, 357 U.S. 116 (1958); Saia v. New York, 334 U.S. 558 (1948); Martin v. City of Struthers, 319 U.S. 141 (1943); Cantwell v. Connecticut, 310 U.S. 296 (1940).
79. Thayer, John Marshall 106–07 (1901).
80. New Republic, June 19, 1961, p. 16.
81. 5 U.S. (1 Cranch) 137 (1803).
82. Ex parte McCardle, 74 U.S. (7 Wall.) 506 (1868).
83. 1 De Tocqueville, Democracy in America 280 (Bradley ed. 1945).
84. 5 U.S. (1 Cranch) 137, 176–78 (1803).
85. Hughes, The Supreme Court of the United States 50 (1928).
86. See id. at 50–54.
87. 75 U.S. (8 Wall.) 603 (1869).
88. 79 U.S. (12 Wall.) 457 (1870).
89. Pollock v. Farmers' Loan & Trust Co., 157 U.S. 429, reargued, 158 U.S. 601 (1895).
90. Compare Jones v. Opelika, 316 U.S. 584 (1942), with Jones v. Opelika, 319 U.S. 103 (1943).
91. Compare Minersville School District v. Gobitis, 310 U.S. 586 (1940), with Board of Educ. v. Barnette, 319 U.S. 624 (1943).
92. 304 U.S. 64 (1938).
93. 60 U.S. (19 How.) 393 (1856).
94. Id. at 588–89.
95. 65 U.S. (24 How.) 66 (1860).
96. 5 U.S. (1 Cranch) 137 (1803).
97. Tietjens v. City of St. Louis, 359 Mo. 439, 443, 222 S.W.2d 70, 72 (1949).
98. Hausner, Individuals' Rights in the Courts of Israel, 1958 International Lawyers Convention In Israel 201, 228 (1959).

99. Handlin & Handlin, The Dimensions of Liberty (1961).

100. Mayo, Hutchinson's History of Massachusetts Bay 415 (1936) (Appendix). See also Aumann, The Instrumentalities of Justice: Their Forms, Functions, and Limitations 84–85 (1956).

101. Stover, The Government of Science (1962).

102. Carson, Silent Spring (1962).

103. See United States ex rel. Carroll v. McNeill, 294 F.2d 117 (2d Cir. 1961), vacated and dismissed as moot, 369 U.S. 149 (1962).

104. Cafeteria Workers v. McElroy, 367 U.S. 886 (1961).

105. Bailey v. Richardson, 182 F.2d 46 (D.C. Cir. 1950).

106. See Beard v. Stahr, 370 U.S. 41 (1962).

107. Orloff v. Willoughby, 345 U.S. 83 (1953).

108. Hurtado v. California, 110 U.S. 516, 531 (1884).

109. Vaughan 135, 124 Eng. Rep. 1006 (C.P. 1670).

110. 217 N.Y. 382, 111 N.E. 1050 (1916). See Prosser, The Assault Upon the Citadel (Strict Liability to the Consumer), 69 Yale L.J. 1099 (1960).

111. Somerset v. Stewart, 20 How. St. Tr. 1, 98 Eng. Rep. 499 (K.B. 1772).

112. Llewellyn, The Common Law Tradition 402 (1960).

113. Betts v. Brady, 316 U.S. 455, 473 (1942).

114. General Electric Forum, Jan.–March 1962, pp. 5–6.

115. The Mind and Faith of A. Powell Davies 151 (Douglas ed. 1959).

116. See Bandy v. United States, 81 Sup. Ct. 197 (1960); 82 Sup. Ct. 11 (1961).

117. See Note, A Study of the Administration of Bail in New York City, 106 U. Pa. L. Rev. 693 (1958).

118. See Ares & Sturz, Bail and the Indigent Accused, 8 Crime & Delinquency 12 (1962).

APPENDIX

The Constitution of the United States of America

W E THE PEOPLE of the United States, in Order to form a more perfect Union, establish Justice, insure domestic Tranquility, provide for the common defence, promote the general Welfare, and secure the Blessings of Liberty to ourselves and our Posterity, do ordain and establish this CONSTITUTION for the United States of America.

ARTICLE I.

SECTION 1. All legislative Powers herein granted shall be vested in a Congress of the United States, which shall consist of a Senate and House of Representatives.

SECTION 2. The House of Representatives shall be composed of Members chosen every second Year by the People of the several States, and the Electors in each State shall have the Qualifications requisite for Electors of the most numerous Branch of the State Legislature.

No Person shall be a Representative who shall not have attained to the Age of twenty-five Years, and been seven Years a Citizen of the United States, and who shall not, when elected, be an Inhabitant of that State in which he shall be chosen.

[Representatives and direct Taxes shall be apportioned among the several States which may be included within this Union, according to their respective Numbers, which shall be determined by adding to the whole Number of free Persons, including those bound to Service for a Term of Years, and excluding Indians not taxed, three fifths of all other Persons.] The actual Enumeration shall be made within three Years after the first Meeting of the Congress of the United States, and within every subsequent Term of ten Years, in such Manner as they shall by Law direct. The Number of Representatives shall not exceed one for every thirty Thousand, but each State shall have at Least one Representative; and until such enumeration shall be made, the State of New Hampshire shall be entitled to chuse three, Massachusetts eight, Rhode-Island and Providence Plantations one, Connecticut five, New-York six, New Jersey four, Pennsylvania eight, Delaware one, Maryland six, Virginia ten, North Carolina five, South Carolina five, and Georgia three.

When vacancies happen in the Representation from any State, the Executive Authority thereof shall issue Writs of Election to fill such Vacancies.

The House of Representatives shall chuse their Speaker and other Officers; and shall have the sole Power of Impeachment.

SECTION 3. The Senate of the United States shall be composed of two Senators from each State, chosen by the Legislature thereof, for six Years; and each Senator shall have one Vote.

Immediately after they shall be assembled in Consequence of the first Election, they shall be divided as equally as may be into three Classes. The Seats of the Senators of the first Class shall be vacated at the Expiration of the second Year, of the second Class at the Expiration of the fourth Year, and of the third Class at the Expiration of the sixth Year, so that one-third may be chosen every second Year; and if Vacancies happen by Resignation, or otherwise, during the Recess of the Legislature of any State, the Executive thereof may make temporary Appointments until the next Meeting of the Legislature, which shall then fill such Vacancies.

No Person shall be a Senator who shall not have attained to the Age of thirty Years, and been nine Years a Citizen of the United States, and who shall not, when elected, be an Inhabitant of that State for which he shall be chosen.

The Vice President of the United States shall be President of the Senate, but shall have no Vote, unless they be equally divided.

The Senate shall chuse their other Officers, and also a President pro tempore, in the absence of the Vice President, or when he shall exercise the Office of President of the United States.

The Senate shall have the sole Power to try all Impeachments. When sitting for that Purpose, they shall be on Oath or Affirmation. When the President of the United States is tried, the Chief Justice shall preside: And no Person shall be convicted without the Concurrence of two thirds of the Members present.

Judgment in Cases of Impeachment shall not extend further than to removal from Office, and disqualification to hold and enjoy any Office of honor, Trust or Profit under the United States: but the Party convicted shall nevertheless be liable and subject to Indictment, Trial, Judgment and Punishment, according to Law.

SECTION 4. The Times, Places and Manner of holding Elections for Senators and Representatives, shall be prescribed in each State by the Legislature thereof; but the Congress may at any time by Law make or alter such Regulations, except as to the Place of Chusing Senators.

The Congress shall assemble at least once in every Year, and such

Meeting shall be on the first Monday in December, unless they shall by Law appoint a different Day.

SECTION 5. Each House shall be the Judge of the Elections, Returns and Qualifications of its own Members, and a Majority of each shall constitute a Quorum to do Business; but a smaller number may adjourn from day to day, and may be authorized to compel the Attendance of absent Members, in such Manner, and under such Penalties as each House may provide.

Each House may determine the Rules of its Proceedings, punish its Members for disorderly Behavior, and, with the Concurrence of two thirds, expel a Member.

Each House shall keep a Journal of its Proceedings, and from time to time publish the same, excepting such Parts as may in their Judgment require Secrecy; and the Yeas and Nays of the Members of either House on any question shall, at the Desire of one fifth of those Present, be entered on the Journal.

Neither House, during the Session of Congress, shall, without the Consent of the other, adjourn for more than three days, nor to any other Place than that in which the two Houses shall be sitting.

SECTION 6. The Senators and Representatives shall receive a Compensation for their Services, to be ascertained by Law, and paid out of the Treasury of the United States. They shall in all Cases, except Treason, Felony and Breach of the Peace, be privileged from Arrest during their Attendance at the Session of their respective Houses, and in going to and returning from the same; and for any Speech or Debate in either House, they shall not be questioned in any other Place.

No Senator or Representative shall, during the Time for which he was elected, be appointed to any civil Office under the Authority of the United States, which shall have been created, or the Emoluments whereof shall have been encreased during such time; and no Person holding any Office under the United States, shall be a Member of either House during his Continuance in Office.

SECTION 7. All Bills for raising Revenue shall originate in the House of Representatives; but the Senate may propose or concur with Amendments as on other Bills.

Every Bill which shall have passed the House of Representatives and the Senate, shall, before it become a Law, be presented to the President of the United States; If he approve he shall sign it, but if not he shall return it, with his Objections to that House in which it shall have originated, who shall enter the Objections at large on their

Journal, and proceed to reconsider it. If after such Reconsideration two thirds of that House shall agree to pass the Bill, it shall be sent, together with the Objections, to the other House, by which it shall likewise be reconsidered, and if approved by two thirds of that House, it shall become a Law. But in all such Cases the Votes of both Houses shall be determined by Yeas and Nays, and the Names of the Persons voting for and against the Bill shall be entered on the Journal of each House respectively. If any Bill shall not be returned by the President within ten Days (Sundays excepted) after it shall have been presented to him, the Same shall be a Law, in like Manner as if he had signed it, unless the Congress by their Adjournment prevent its Return, in which Case it shall not be a Law.

Every Order, Resolution, or Vote to which the Concurrence of the Senate and House of Representatives may be necessary (except on a question of Adjournment) shall be presented to the President of the United States; and before the Same shall take Effect, shall be approved by him, or being disapproved by him, shall be repassed by two thirds of the Senate and House of Representatives, according to the Rules and Limitations prescribed in the Case of a Bill.

SECTION 8. The Congress shall have Power To lay and collect Taxes, Duties, Imposts and Excises, to pay the Debts and provide for the common Defence and general Welfare of the United States; but all Duties, Imposts and Excises shall be uniform throughout the United States;

To borrow money on the credit of the United States;

To regulate Commerce with foreign Nations, and among the several States, and with the Indian Tribes;

To establish an uniform Rule of Naturalization, and uniform Laws on the subject of Bankruptcies throughout the United States;

To coin Money, regulate the Value thereof, and of foreign Coin, and fix the Standard of Weights and Measures;

To provide for the Punishment of counterfeiting the Securities and current Coin of the United States;

To establish Post Offices and post Roads;

To promote the Progress of Science and useful Arts, by securing for limited Times to Authors and Inventors the exclusive Right to their respective Writings and Discoveries;

To constitute Tribunals inferior to the supreme Court;

To define and punish Piracies and Felonies committed on the high Seas, and Offenses against the Law of Nations;

To declare War, grant Letters of Marque and Reprisal, and make Rules concerning Captures on Land and Water;

To raise and support Armies, but no Appropriation of Money to that Use shall be for a longer Term than two Years;

To provide and maintain a Navy;

To make Rules for the Government and Regulation of the land and naval Forces;

To provide for calling forth the Militia to execute the Laws of the Union, suppress Insurrections and repel Invasions;

To provide for organizing, arming, and disciplining the Militia, and for governing such Part of them as may be employed in the Service of the United States, reserving to the States respectively, the Appointment of the Officers, and the Authority of training the Militia according to the discipline prescribed by Congress;

To exercise exclusive Legislation in all Cases whatsoever, over such District (not exceeding ten Miles square) as may, by Cession of particular States, and the acceptance of Congress, become the Seat of the Government of the United States, and to exercise like Authority over all Places purchased by the Consent of the Legislature of the State in which the Same shall be, for the Erection of Forts, Magazines, Arsenals, dock-Yards, and other needful Buildings;—And

To make all Laws which shall be necessary and proper for carrying into Execution the foregoing Powers, and all other Powers vested by this Constitution in the Government of the United States, or in any Department or Officer thereof.

SECTION 9. The Migration or Importation of such Persons as any of the States now existing shall think proper to admit, shall not be prohibited by the Congress prior to the Year one thousand eight hundred and eight, but a tax or duty may be imposed on such Importation, not exceeding ten dollars for each Person.

The privilege of the Writ of Habeas Corpus shall not be suspended, unless when in Cases of Rebellion or Invasion the public Safety may require it.

No Bill of Attainder or ex post facto Law shall be passed.

No capitation, or other direct, Tax shall be laid, unless in Proportion to the Census or Enumeration herein before directed to be taken.

No Tax or Duty shall be laid on Articles exported from any State.

No Preference shall be given by any Regulation of Commerce or

Revenue to the Ports of one State over those of another: nor shall Vessels bound to, or from, one State, be obliged to enter, clear, or pay Duties in another.

No Money shall be drawn from the Treasury, but in Consequence of Appropriations made by Law; and a regular Statement and Account of the Receipts and Expenditures of all public Money shall be published from time to time.

No Title of Nobility shall be granted by the United States: And no Person holding any Office of Profit or Trust under them, shall, without the Consent of the Congress, accept of any present, Emolument, Office, or Title, of any kind whatever, from any King, Prince, or foreign State.

SECTION 10. No State shall enter into any Treaty, Alliance, or Confederation; grant Letters of Marque and Reprisal; coin Money; emit Bills of Credit; make any Thing but gold and silver Coin a Tender in Payment of Debts; pass any Bill of Attainder, ex post facto Law, or Law impairing the Obligation of Contracts, or grant any Title of Nobility.

No State shall, without the Consent of the Congress, lay any Imposts or Duties on Imports or Exports, except what may be absolutely necessary for executing it's inspection Laws: and the net Produce of all Duties and Imposts, laid by any State on Imports or Exports, shall be for the Use of the Treasury of the United States; and all such Laws shall be subject to the Revision and Controul of the Congress.

No State shall, without the Consent of Congress, lay any duty of Tonnage, keep Troops, or Ships of War in time of Peace, enter into any Agreement or Compact with another State, or with a foreign Power, or engage in War, unless actually invaded, or in such imminent Danger as will not admit of delay.

ARTICLE II.

SECTION 1. The Executive Power shall be vested in a President of the United States of America. He shall hold his Office during the Term of four Years, and, together with the Vice-President, chosen for the same Term, be elected, as follows

Each State shall appoint, in such Manner as the Legislature thereof may direct, a Number of Electors, equal to the whole Number of Senators and Representatives to which the State may be entitled in the Congress: but no Senator or Representative, or Person holding an

Office of Trust or Profit under the United States, shall be appointed an Elector.

[The Electors shall meet in their respective States, and vote by Ballot for two persons, of whom one at least shall not be an Inhabitant of the same State with themselves. And they shall make a List of all the Persons voted for, and of the Number of Votes for each; which List they shall sign and certify, and transmit sealed to the Seat of the Government of the United States, directed to the President of the Senate. The President of the Senate shall, in the Presence of the Senate and House of Representatives, open all the Certificates, and the Votes shall then be counted. The Person having the greatest Number of Votes shall be the President, if such Number be a Majority of the whole Number of Electors appointed; and if there be more than one who have such Majority, and have an equal Number of Votes, then the House of Representatives shall immediately chuse by Ballot one of them for President; and if no Person have a Majority, then from the five highest on the List the said House shall in like Manner chuse the President. But in chusing the President, the Votes shall be taken by States, the Representation from each State having one Vote; A quorum for this Purpose shall consist of a Member or Members from two-thirds of the States, and a Majority of all the States shall be necessary to a Choice. In every Case, after the Choice of the President, the Person having the greatest Number of Votes of the Electors shall be the Vice President. But if there should remain two or more who have equal Votes, the Senate shall chuse from them by Ballot the Vice-President.]

The Congress may determine the Time of chusing the Electors, and the Day on which they shall give their Votes; which Day shall be the same throughout the United States.

No person except a natural born Citizen, or a Citizen of the United States, at the time of the Adoption of this Constitution, shall be eligible to the Office of President; neither shall any Person be eligible to that Office who shall not have attained to the Age of thirty-five Years, and been fourteen Years a Resident within the United States.

In Case of the Removal of the President from Office, or of his Death, Resignation, or Inability to discharge the Powers and Duties of the said Office, the same shall devolve on the Vice President, and the Congress may by Law provide for the Case of Removal, Death, Resignation or Inability, both of the President and Vice President, declaring what Officer shall then act as President, and such Officer shall act accordingly, until the Disability be removed, or a President shall be elected.

The President shall, at stated Times, receive for his Services, a Compensation, which shall neither be encreased nor diminished during the Period for which he shall have been elected, and he shall not receive within that Period any other Emolument from the United States, or any of them.

Before he enter on the Execution of his Office, he shall take the following Oath or Affirmation:—"I do solemnly swear (or affirm) that I will faithfully execute the Office of President of the United States, and will to the best of my Ability, preserve, protect and defend the Constitution of the United States."

SECTION 2. The President shall be Commander in Chief of the Army and Navy of the United States, and of the Militia of the several States, when called into the actual Service of the United States; he may require the Opinion in writing, of the principal Officer in each of the executive Departments, upon any subject relating to the Duties of their respective Offices, and he shall have Power to Grant Reprieves and Pardons for Offenses against the United States, except in Cases of Impeachment.

He shall have Power, by and with the Advice and Consent of the Senate, to make Treaties, provided two-thirds of the Senators present concur; and he shall nominate, and by and with the Advice and Consent of the Senate, shall appoint Ambassadors, other public Ministers and Consuls, Judges of the supreme Court, and all other Officers of the United States, whose Appointments are not herein otherwise provided for, and which shall be established by Law: but the Congress may by Law vest the Appointment of such inferior Officers, as they think proper, in the President alone, in the Courts of Law, or in the Heads of Departments.

The President shall have Power to fill up all Vacancies that may happen during the Recess of the Senate, by granting Commissions which shall expire at the End of their next Session.

SECTION 3. He shall from time to time give to the Congress Information of the State of the Union, and recommend to their Consideration such Measures as he shall judge necessary and expedient; he may, on extraordinary Occasions, convene both Houses, or either of them, and in Case of Disagreement between them, with Respect to the Time of Adjournment, he may adjourn them to such Time as he shall think proper; he shall receive Ambassadors and other public Ministers; he shall take Care that the Laws be faithfully executed, and shall Commission all the Officers of the United States.

Section 4. The President, Vice President and all civil Officers of the United States, shall be removed from Office on Impeachment for, and Conviction of, Treason, Bribery, or other high Crimes and Misdemeanors.

ARTICLE III.

Section 1. The judicial Power of the United States, shall be vested in one supreme Court, and in such inferior Courts as the Congress may from time to time ordain and establish. The Judges, both of the supreme and inferior Courts, shall hold their Offices during good Behaviour, and shall, at stated Times, receive for their Services a Compensation which shall not be diminished during their Continuance in Office.

Section 2. The judicial Power shall extend to all Cases, in Law and Equity, arising under this Constitution, the Laws of the United States, and Treaties made, or which shall be made, under their Authority;—to all Cases affecting Ambassadors, other public Ministers and Consuls;—to all Cases of admiralty and maritime Jurisdiction;—to Controversies to which the United States shall be a Party;—to Controversies between two or more States;—between a State and Citizens of another State;—between Citizens of different States;—between Citizens of the same State claiming Lands under Grants of different States, and between a State, or the Citizens thereof, and foreign States, Citizens or Subjects.

In all Cases affecting Ambassadors, other public Ministers and Consuls, and those in which a State shall be Party, the supreme Court shall have original Jurisdiction. In all the other Cases before mentioned, the supreme Court shall have appellate Jurisdiction, both as to Law and Fact, with such Exceptions, and under such Regulations as the Congress shall make.

The trial of all Crimes, except in Cases of Impeachment, shall be by Jury; and such Trial shall be held in the State where the said Crimes shall have been committed; but when not committed within any State, the Trial shall be at such Place or Places as the Congress may by Law have directed.

Section 3. Treason against the United States, shall consist only in levying War against them, or in adhering to their Enemies, giving them Aid and Comfort. No Person shall be convicted of Treason unless on the Testimony of two Witnesses to the same overt Act, or on Confession in open Court.

The Congress shall have power to declare the Punishment of Treason, but no Attainder of Treason shall work Corruption of Blood, or Forfeiture except during the Life of the Person attainted.

ARTICLE IV.

SECTION 1. Full Faith and Credit shall be given in each State to the public Acts, Records, and judicial Proceedings of every other State. And the Congress may by general Laws prescribe the Manner in which such Acts, Records and Proceedings shall be proved, and the Effect thereof.

SECTION 2. The Citizens of each State shall be entitled to all Privileges and Immunities of Citizens in the several States.

A Person charged in any State with Treason, Felony, or other Crime, who shall flee from Justice, and be found in another State, shall on demand of the executive Authority of the State from which he fled, be delivered up, to be removed to the State having Jurisdiction of the Crime.

No Person held to Service or Labour in one State, under the Laws thereof, escaping into another, shall, in Consequence of any Law or Regulation therein, be discharged from such Service or Labour, but shall be delivered up on Claim of the Party to whom such Service or Labour may be due.

SECTION 3. New States may be admitted by the Congress into this Union; but no new States shall be formed or erected within the Jurisdiction of any other State; nor any State be formed by the Junction of two or more States, or parts of States, without the Consent of the Legislatures of the States concerned as well as of the Congress.

The Congress shall have Power to dispose of and make all needful Rules and Regulations respecting the Territory or other Property belonging to the United States; and nothing in this Constitution shall be so construed as to Prejudice any Claims of the United States, or of any particular State.

SECTION 4. The United States shall guarantee to every State in this Union a Republican Form of Government, and shall protect each of them against Invasion; and on Application of the Legislature, or of the Executive (when the Legislature cannot be convened) against domestic Violence.

ARTICLE V.

The Congress, whenever two-thirds of both Houses shall deem it necessary, shall propose Amendments to this Constitution, or, on the Application of the Legislatures of two-thirds of the several States, shall call a Convention for proposing amendments, which, in either Case, shall be valid to all Intents and Purposes, as part of this Constitution, when ratified by the Legislatures of three-fourths of the several States, or by Conventions in three-fourths thereof, as the one or the other Mode of Ratification may be proposed by the Congress; Provided that no Amendment which may be made prior to the Year One thousand eight hundred and eight shall in any Manner affect the first and fourth Clauses in the Ninth Section of the first Article; and that no State, without its Consent, shall be deprived of its equal Suffrage in the Senate.

ARTICLE VI.

All Debts contracted and Engagements entered into, before the Adoption of this Constitution, shall be as valid against the United States under this Constitution, as under the Confederation.

This Constitution, and the Laws of the United States which shall be made in Pursuance thereof; and all Treaties made, or which shall be made, under the Authority of the United States, shall be the supreme Law of the Land; and the Judges in every State shall be bound thereby, any Thing in the Constitution or Laws of any State to the Contrary notwithstanding.

The Senators and Representatives before mentioned, and the Members of the several State Legislatures, and all executive and judicial Officers, both of the United States and of the several States, shall be bound by Oath or Affirmation, to support this Constitution; but no religious Test shall ever be required as a Qualification to any Office or public Trust under the United States.

ARTICLE VII.

The Ratification of the Conventions of nine States shall be sufficient for the Establishment of this Constitution between the States so ratifying the Same.

DONE in Convention by the Unanimous Consent of the States present the Seventeenth Day of September in the Year of our Lord one thousand seven hundred and Eighty seven and of the Inde-

189

pendence of the United States of America the Twelfth. In Witness whereof We have hereunto subscribed our Names.

G<u>o</u> WASHINGTON
Presidt and deputy from Virginia

New Hampshire.

JOHN LANGDON
NICHOLAS GILMAN

Massachusetts.

NATHANIEL GORHAM
RUFUS KING

Connecticut.

WM SAML JOHNSON
ROGER SHERMAN

New York.

ALEXANDER HAMILTON

New Jersey.

WIL: LIVINGSTON
DAVID BREARLEY.
WM PATTERSON
JONA: DAYTON

Pennsylvania.

B. FRANKLIN
ROBT. MORRIS
THOS. FITZSIMONS
JAMES WILSON
THOMAS MIFFLIN
GEO. CLYMER
JARED INGERSOLL
GOUV MORRIS

Delaware.

GEO: READ
JOHN DICKINSON
JACO: BROOM
GUNNING BEDFORD jun
RICHARD BASSETT

Maryland.

JAMES MCHENRY
DANL CARROLL
DAN: of ST THOS JENIFER

Virginia.

JOHN BLAIR—
JAMES MADISON Jr.

North Carolina.

WM BLOUNT
HU WILLIAMSON
RICHD DOBBS SPAIGHT,

South Carolina.

J. RUTLEDGE
CHARLES PINCKNEY
CHARLES COTESWORTH PINCKNEY
PIERCE BUTLER.

Georgia.

WILLIAM FEW
ABR BALDWIN

Attest:

WILLIAM JACKSON, *Secretary.*

ARTICLES IN ADDITION TO, AND AMENDMENT OF, THE CONSTITUTION OF THE UNITED STATES OF AMERICA, PROPOSED BY CONGRESS, AND RATIFIED BY THE LEGISLATURES OF THE SEVERAL STATES, PURSUANT TO THE FIFTH ARTICLE OF THE ORIGINAL CONSTITUTION.

ARTICLE I.

Congress shall make no law respecting an establishment of religion, or prohibiting the free exercise thereof; or abridging the freedom of speech, or of the press; or the right of the people peaceably to assemble, and to petition the Government for a redress of grievances.

ARTICLE II.

A well regulated Militia, being necessary to the security of a free State, the right of the people to keep and bear Arms, shall not be infringed.

ARTICLE III.

No Soldier shall, in time of peace be quartered in any house, without the consent of the Owner, nor in time of war, but in a manner to be prescribed by law.

ARTICLE IV.

The right of the people to be secure in their persons, houses, papers, and effects, against unreasonable searches and seizures, shall not be violated, and no Warrants shall issue, but upon probable cause, supported by Oath or affirmation, and particularly describing the place to be searched, and the persons or things to be seized.

ARTICLE V.

No person shall be held to answer for a capital, or otherwise infamous crime, unless on a presentment or indictment of a Grand Jury, except in cases arising in the land or naval forces, or in the Militia, when in actual service in time of War or public danger; nor shall any person be subject for the same offence to be twice put in jeopardy of life or limb; nor shall be compelled in any criminal case to be a witness against himself, nor be deprived of life, liberty, or property, without due process of law; nor shall private property be taken for public use, without just compensation.

ARTICLE VI.

In all criminal prosecutions, the accused shall enjoy the right to a speedy and public trial, by an impartial jury of the State and district wherein the crime shall have been committed, which district shall have been previously ascertained by law, and to be informed of the nature and cause of the accusation; to be confronted with the witnesses against him; to have compulsory process for obtaining witnesses in his favor, and to have the Assistance of Counsel for his defence.

ARTICLE VII.

In suits at common law, where the value in controversy shall exceed twenty dollars, the right of trial by jury shall be preserved, and no fact tried by a jury, shall be otherwise re-examined in any Court of the United States, than according to the rules of the common law.

ARTICLE VIII.

Excessive bail shall not be required, nor excessive fines imposed, nor cruel and unusual punishments inflicted.

ARTICLE IX.

The enumeration in the Constitution, of certain rights, shall not be construed to deny or disparage others retained by the people.

ARTICLE X.

The powers not delegated to the United States by the Constitution, nor prohibited by it to the States, are reserved to the States respectively, or to the people.

ARTICLE XI.

The Judicial power of the United States shall not be construed to extend to any suit in law or equity, commenced or prosecuted against one of the United States by Citizens of another State, or by Citizens or Subjects of any Foreign State.

ARTICLE XII.

The Electors shall meet in their respective states and vote by ballot for President and Vice-President, one of whom, at least, shall not be an inhabitant of the same state with themselves; they shall name in their ballots the person voted for as President, and in distinct ballots the person voted for as Vice-President, and they shall make distinct lists of all persons voted for as President, and of all persons voted for as Vice-President, and of the number of votes for each, which lists they shall sign and certify, and transmit sealed to the seat of the government of the United States, directed to the President of the Senate;—The President of the Senate shall, in presence of the Senate and House of Representatives, open all the certificates and the votes shall then be counted;—The person having the greatest number of votes for President, shall be the President, if such number be a majority of the whole number of Electors appointed; and if no person have such majority, then from the persons having the highest numbers not exceeding three on the list of those voted for as President, the House of Representatives shall choose immediately, by ballot, the President. But in choosing the President, the votes shall be taken by states, the representation from each state having one vote; a quorum for this purpose shall consist of a member or members from two-thirds of the states, and a majority of all the states shall be necessary to a choice. And if the House of Representatives shall not choose a President whenever the right of choice shall devolve upon them, before the fourth day of March next following, then the Vice-President shall act as President, as in the case of the death or other constitutional disability of the President.—The person having the greatest number of votes as Vice-President, shall be the Vice-President, if such number be a majority of the whole number of Electors appointed, and if no person have a majority, then from the two highest numbers on the list, the Senate shall choose the Vice-President; a quorum for the purpose shall consist of two-thirds of the whole number of Senators, and a majority of the whole number shall be necessary to a choice. But no person constitutionally ineligible to the office of President shall be eligible to that of Vice-President of the United States.

ARTICLE XIII.

SECTION 1. Neither slavery nor involuntary servitude, except as a punishment for crime whereof the party shall have been duly convicted, shall exist within the United States, or any place subject to their jurisdiction.

SECTION 2. Congress shall have power to enforce this article by appropriate legislation.

ARTICLE XIV.

SECTION 1. All persons born or naturalized in the United States, and subject to the jurisdiction thereof, are citizens of the United States and of the State wherein they reside. No State shall make or enforce any law which shall abridge the privileges or immunities of citizens of the United States; nor shall any State deprive any person of life, liberty, or property, without due process of law; nor deny to any person within its jurisdiction the equal protection of the laws.

SECTION 2. Representatives shall be apportioned among the several States according to their respective numbers, counting the whole number of persons in each State, excluding Indians not taxed. But when the right to vote at any election for the choice of electors for President and Vice-President of the United States, Representatives in Congress, the Executive and Judicial officers of a State, or the members of the Legislature thereof, is denied to any of the male inhabitants of such State, being twenty-one years of age, and citizens of the United States, or in any way abridged, except for participation in rebellion, or other crime, the basis of representation therein shall be reduced in the proportion which the number of such male citizens shall bear to the whole number of male citizens twenty-one years of age in such State.

SECTION 3. No person shall be a Senator or Representative in Congress, or elector of President and Vice-President, or hold any office, civil or military, under the United States, or under any State, who, having previously taken an oath, as a member of Congress, or as an officer of the United States, or as a member of any State legislature, or as an executive or judicial officer of any State, to support the Constitution of the United States, shall have engaged in insurrection or rebellion against the same, or given aid or comfort to the enemies thereof. But Congress may by a vote of two-thirds of each House, remove such disability.

SECTION 4. The validity of the public debt of the United States, authorized by law, including debts incurred for payment of pensions and bounties for services in suppressing insurrection or rebellion, shall not be questioned. But neither the United States nor any State shall assume or pay any debt or obligation incurred in aid of insurrection or rebellion against the United States, or any claim for the loss or emancipation of any slave; but all such debts, obligations and claims shall be held illegal and void.

Section 5. The Congress shall have power to enforce, by appropriate legislation, the provisions of this article.

ARTICLE XV.

Section 1. The right of citizens of the United States to vote shall not be denied or abridged by the United States or by any State on account of race, color, or previous condition of servitude—

Section 2. The Congress shall have power to enforce this article by appropriate legislation.

ARTICLE XVI.

The Congress shall have power to lay and collect taxes on incomes, from whatever source derived, without apportionment among the several States, and without regard to any census or enumeration.

ARTICLE XVII.

The Senate of the United States shall be composed of two Senators from each State, elected by the people thereof, for six years; and each Senator shall have one vote. The electors in each State shall have the qualifications requisite for electors of the most numerous branch of the State legislatures.

When vacancies happen in the representation of any State in the Senate, the executive authority of such State shall issue writs of election to fill such vacancies: *Provided*, That the legislature of any State may empower the executive thereof to make temporary appointments until the people fill the vacancies by election as the legislature may direct.

This amendment shall not be so construed as to affect the election or term of any Senator chosen before it becomes valid as part of the Constitution.

ARTICLE XVIII.

Section 1. After one year from the ratification of this article the manufacture, sale, or transportation of intoxicating liquors within, the importation thereof into, or the exportation thereof from the

United States and all territory subject to the jurisdiction thereof for beverage purposes is hereby prohibited.

SECTION 2. The Congress and the several States shall have concurrent power to enforce this article by appropriate legislation.

SECTION 3. This article shall be inoperative unless it shall have been ratified as an amendment to the Constitution by the legislatures of the several States, as provided in the Constitution, within seven years from the date of the submission hereof to the States by the Congress.

ARTICLE XIX.

The right of citizens of the United States to vote shall not be denied or abridged by the United States or by any State on account of sex.

Congress shall have power to enforce this article by appropriate legislation.

ARTICLE XX.

SECTION 1. The terms of the President and Vice President shall end at noon on the 20th day of January, and the terms of Senators and Representatives at noon on the 3d day of January, of the years in which such terms would have ended if this article had not been ratified; and the terms of their successors shall then begin.

SECTION 2. The Congress shall assemble at least once in every year, and such meeting shall begin at noon on the 3d day of January, unless they shall by law appoint a different day.

SECTION 3. If, at the time fixed for the beginning of the term of the President, the President elect shall have died, the Vice President elect shall become President. If a President shall not have been chosen before the time fixed for the beginning of his term, or if the President elect shall have failed to qualify, then the Vice President elect shall act as President until a President shall have qualified; and the Congress may by law provide for the case wherein neither a President elect nor a Vice President elect shall have qualified, declaring who shall then act as President, or the manner in which one who is to act shall be selected, and such person shall act accordingly until a President or Vice President shall have qualified.

SECTION 4. The Congress may by law provide for the case of the death of any of the persons from whom the House of Representatives may choose a President whenever the right of choice shall have devolved upon them, and for the case of the death of any of the persons from whom the Senate may choose a Vice President whenever the right of choice shall have devolved upon them.

SECTION 5. Sections 1 and 2 shall take effect on the 15th day of October following the ratification of this article.

SECTION 6. This article shall be inoperative unless it shall have been ratified as an amendment to the Constitution by the legislatures of three-fourths of the several States within seven years from the date of its submission.

ARTICLE XXI.

SECTION 1. The eighteenth article of amendment to the Constitution of the United States is hereby repealed.

SECTION 2. The transportation or importation into any State, Territory, or possession of the United States for delivery or use therein of intoxicating liquors, in violation of the laws thereof, is hereby prohibited.

SECTION 3. This article shall be inoperative unless it shall have been ratified as an amendment to the Constitution by conventions in the several States, as provided in the Constitution, within seven years from the date of the submission hereof to the States by the Congress.

ARTICLE XXII

SECTION 1. No person shall be elected to the office of the President more than twice, and no person who has held the office of President, or acted as President, for more than two years of a term to which some other person was elected President shall be elected to the office of the President more than once. But this Article shall not apply to any person holding the office of President when this Article was proposed by the Congress, and shall not prevent any person who may be holding the office of President, or acting as President, during the term within which this Article becomes operative from holding the office of President or acting as President during the remainder of such term.

SECTION 2. This article shall be inoperative unless it shall have been ratified as an amendment to the Constitution by the legislatures of three-fourths of the several States within seven years from the date of its submission to the States by the Congress.

ABOUT THE CONTRIBUTORS

HUGO L. BLACK is senior Associate Justice of the United States Supreme Court. Born in 1886 at Harlan, Alabama, he served ten years as United States Senator from Alabama before his appointment to the Court in 1937.

IRVING BRANT, born in 1885 at Walker, Iowa, is the author of the definitive *James Madison* (six volumes, published 1941–1961), which many consider the most influential American biography of the century.

WILLIAM J. BRENNAN, JR. is Associate Justice of the United States Supreme Court. Born in 1906 at Newark, New Jersey, he served seven years on the New Jersey bench before his appointment to the Court in 1956.

EDMOND CAHN, born in 1906 at New Orleans, Louisiana, is Professor of Law at New York University. His latest book is *The Predicament of Democratic Man*.

WILLIAM O. DOUGLAS is Associate Justice of the United States Supreme Court. Born in 1898 at Maine, Minnesota, he served three years as commissioner and chairman of the Securities and Exchange Commission before his appointment to the Court in 1939.

EARL WARREN is Chief Justice of the United States. Born in 1891 at Los Angeles, California, he served ten years as governor of California before his appointment to the Court in 1953.

ACKNOWLEDGMENTS

I take pleasure in extending hearty thanks to the kind colleagues who assisted in making this volume possible. Among them are Dean Russell D. Niles and Professor Harry J. Rudick, whose constant encouragement and warm support deserve the very highest commendation.

Let me also acknowledge my indebtedness and express my gratitude to Burt Pines and Roger W. Thomas, senior students at the School of Law, for preparing the following tables and index and for rendering excellent assistance in regard to my editorial chores.

—The Editor

TABLE OF CASES

Abel v. United States, 362 U.S. 217 (1960): *169, 172*

Adamson v. California, 332 U.S. 46 (1947): *44, 75, 164*

Aetna Life Ins. Co. v. Haworth, 300 U.S. 227 (1937): *173*

Alcorta v. Texas, 235 U.S. 28 (1957): *165*

Ashby v. White, 2 Ld. Raym. 938, 92 Eng. Rep. 126 (K.B. 1702):*136*

Associated Industries Inc. v. Ickes, 134 F.2d 694 (1943): *173*

Baker v. Carr, 369 U.S. 186 (1962): *137*

Bailey v. Richardson, 182 F.2d 46 (D.C. Cir. 1950): *175*

Bandy v. United States, 81 Sup. Ct. 197 (1960); 82 Sup. Ct. 11 (1961): *172, 175*

Barron v. Baltimore, 32 U.S.(7 Pet.) 242 (1833): *44, 71*

Bartkus v. Illinois, 359 U.S. 121 (1959): *166*

Beard v. Stahr, 370 U.S. 41 (1962): *175*

Beauharnais v. Illinois, 343 U.S. 250 (1952): *165*

Bell v. United States, 366 U.S. 393 (1961): *170*

Bell v. United States, 181 F. Supp. 668 (Ct. Cl. 1960): *170*

Betts v. Brady, 316 U.S. 455 (1942): *165, 173, 175*

Board of Educ. v. Barnette, 319 U.S. 624 (1943): *174*

Breithaupt v. Abram, 352 U.S. 432 (1957): *132*

Bridges v. California, 314 U.S. 252 (1941): *164*

Brown v. Mississippi, 297 U.S. 278 (1936): *165*

Buchanan v. Warley, 245 U.S. 60 (1917): *174*

Burns v. Wilson, 346 U.S. 137 (1953): *97*

Bushell's Case, Vaughan 135, 124 Eng. Rep. 1006 (C.P. 1670): *150*

Cafeteria Workers v. McElroy, 367 U.S. 886 (1961): *110, 175*

Cantwell v. Connecticut, 310 U.S. 296 (1940): *164, 174*

Carlson v. Landon, 342 U.S. 524 (1952): *130*

Chicago & So. Air Lines, Inc. v. Waterman S.S. Corp., 333 U.S. 103 (1948): *135*

Chicago, B. & Q. R.R. v. Chicago, 166 U.S. 226 (1897): *165*

City of Atlanta v. Ickes, 308 U.S. 517 (1939) (per curiam): *173*

Ciucci v. Illinois, 356 U.S. 571 (1958): *165*

Cole v. Young, 351 U.S. 536 (1956): *171*

TABLE OF SOURCES

Adams, The Jubilee of the Constitution (1839): 68

Administrative Procedure Act § 10(a), 60 Stat. 243 (1946), 5 U.S.C. § 1009(a) (1958): 173

1960 Adm'r of Veterans' Affairs Ann. Rep. (1961): 167

1 Annals of Cong. (1834): 160, 161, 162, 163, 165, 166

3 Annals of Cong. (1834): 162

Ares & Sturz, Bail and the Indigent Accused, 8 Crime & Delinquency 12 (1962): 175

Ark. H.B. 111, introduced Jan. 17, 1961 (Proposed): 166

Aumann, The Instrumentalities of Justice: Their Forms, Functions, and Limitations (1956): 175

Bagehot, The English Constitution (2d ed. 1873): 172

Beinart, The South African Appeal Court and Judicial Review, 21 Modern L. Rev. 578 (1958): 172

Brief for Petitioner, The Secretary of Defense, McElroy v. United States ex rel. Guargliardo, 361 U.S. 281 (1960): 169

Burnett, Letters of Members of the Continental Congress (1933): 160

Cardozo, The Nature of the Judicial Process (1921): 165

Carson, Silent Spring (1962): 149

Chafee, Free Speech in the United States (1948): 130

Channing, A History of the United States (1912): 92

Complete Works of Abraham Lincoln (Nicolay & Hay ed. 1894): 200

87 Cong. Rec. 555 (1941): 168

96 Cong. Rec. 14835, 14919, 15177, A6561 (1950): 167

Czechoslovak Law No. 140/1961 Coll. on Instigation, § 100(1), (2) (Jan. 1, 1962): 172

Dash, The Eavesdroppers (1959): 172

Dep't of the Army Pamphlet No. 27–101–18 (Oct. 7, 1959), reprinted in 1960 U.S.C.M.A. Ann. Rep. 4: 168

DeTocqueville, Democracy in America (Bradley ed. 1945): 117, 124, 126, 142

Diary and Autobiography of John Adams (Butterfield ed. 1961): 127

Documents Illustrative of Formation of the Union of American States, H.R. Doc. No. 398, 69th Cong., 1st Sess. 1018–20, 1024–44 (1927): *167*

Douglas, Vagrancy and Arrest on Suspicion, 70 Yale L.J. 1 (1960). *166*

Dumbauld, The Bill of Rights and What it Means Today (1957): *163, 164*

Elliot's Debates (2d ed. 1836): *159, 172*

Fairman, Does the Fourteenth Amendment Incorporate the Bill of Rights?—The Original Understanding, 2 Stan. L. Rev. 5 (1949): *163*

The Federalist (Lodge ed. 1891): *29, 30, 163, 166*

The Federalist (Wright ed. 1961): *172*

Flack, The Adoption of the Fourteenth Amendment (1908): *164*

Frankfurter, Law and Politics (1939): *172, 173*

Freeman, George Washington (1952): *166*

General Elec. Forum, Jan.-March, ch. 1962, pp. 5–6: *175*

Gwathmey, Twelve Virginia Counties (1937): *160*

Handlin & Handlin, The Dimensions of Liberty (1961): *147*

Harris, The Constitutional Crisis in South Africa, 103 Sol. J. 995 (1959): *172*

Hausner, Individuals' Rights in the Courts of Israel, 1958 International Lawyers' Convention in Israel 201 (1959): *146*

Holdsworth, A History of English Law (1924): *173*

H.R. Doc. No. 986, 76th Cong., 3d Sess. 2, 3, 11 (1940): *173*

Hughes, The Supreme Court of the United States (1928): *144*

Ill. Ann. Stat. ch. 38, § 601.1 (Smith-Hurd Supp. 1960): *166*

Jefferson, Writings (Washington ed. 1859): *63, 162*

Lacy, Freedom and Communications (1961): *126*

Landis, South African Apartheid Legislation II: Extension, Enforcement and Perpetuation, 71 Yale L.J. 437 (1962): *172*

Letter from James Madison to Thomas Jefferson, Oct. 17, 1788: *4*

Letter from Mathew Carey to James Madison, Oct. 30, 1814, reprinted in Papers of James Madison, Library of Congress: *38*

Leveller Manifestoes of the Puritan Revolution (Wolfe ed. 1944): *162*

Levy, Legacy of Suppression (1960): *172*

Llewellyn, The Common Law Tradition (1960): *112*

Madison, Notes of the Debates in the Federal Convention of 1787 (Hunt-Scott ed. 1920): *161*

Mayo, Hutchinson's History of Massachusetts Bay (1936): *175*

Meiklejohn, Book Review, 35 So. Cal. L. Rev. 111 (1961): *172*

Miller, The Legal Mind in America from Independence to the Civil War (1962): *159*

The Mind and Faith of A. Powell Davies (Douglas ed. 1959): *175*

Morrison, Does the Fourteenth Amendment Incorporate the Bill of Rights?—The Judicial Interpretation, 2 Stan. L. Rev. 140 (1949): *164*

Nat'l Office of Vital Statistics, Life Tables § 5–5 (Dep't of Health, Educ. & Welfare 1959): *167*

Navy Judge Advocate General Admiral Mott, An Appraisal of Proposed Changes in the Uniform Code of Military Justice, 35 St. John's L. Rev. 300 (1961): *168*

New Republic, June 19, 1961, p. 16: *174*

N.Y. Times, March 29, 1961, p. 16, cols. 1, 2: *170–71*

N.Y. Times, May 21, 1961, p. 48, cols. 4–5: *171*

N.Y. Times, Jan. 18, 1961, p. 22, cols. 5, 6: *171*

Note, A Study of the Administration of Bail in New York City, 106 U. Pa. L. Rev. 693 (1958): *156*

Note, The Void-For-Vagueness Doctrine in the Supreme Court, 109 U. Pa. L. Rev. 67 (1960): *174*

N. W. Ayre & Son, Directory of Newspapers and Periodicals (1942) (1952) (1962): *172*

Office of the Secretary of Defense, Pamphlet 22.1 (Dec. 20, 1961): *167*

Papers of Thomas Jefferson (Boyd ed. 1958): *173*

Prosser, The Assault upon the Citadel (Strict Liability to the Consumer), 69 Yale L.J. 1099 (1960): *175*

1945 Public Papers of the Presidents of the United States: Harry S Truman (1961): *171*

Quinn, The United States Court of Military Appeals and Military Due Process, 35 St. John's L. Rev. 225 (1961): *168*

Rawle, A View of the Constitution of the United States of America (1825): *70, 80*

Records of the Federal Convention (Farrand ed. 1911): *167*

Report of Secretary of War Knox to the Congress, Aug. 10, 1789, 1 American State Papers—Military Affairs No. 1: *167*

Rives, History of the Life and Times of James Madison (1859–1866): *161, 162*

Schaefer, Federalism and State Criminal Procedure, 70 Harv. L. Rev. 1 (1956): *84*

Senate Comm. on Armed Services, Operation of Article VII, NATO Status of Forces Treaty, S. Rep. No. 1041, 87th Cong., 1st Sess. 2 (1961): *168*

Stover, The Government of Science (1962): *148*

Tansill, Documents Illustrative of the Formation of the Union (1927): *160*

Tex. Code Crim. Proc. art. 494 (Supp. 1960): *166*

Thayer, John Marshall (1901): *174*

Truman, Memoirs (1956): *171*

Uniform Code of Military Justice, 10 U.S.C. 867, 876 (1958): 97

28 U.S.C. § 2254 (1958): *173*

U.S. Dep't of Commerce, Statistical Abstract of the United States (1961): *170–71*

U.S. Dep't of State, Treaties in Force (Jan. 1, 1962): *168*

Universal Military Training and Service Act of 1951, §§ 4(b), (d), 65 Stat. 78 (1951), as amended, 50 U.S.C. App. §§ 454(b), (d), (1958): *167*

Warren, The Making of the Constitution (1929): *159*

Washington National Intelligencer, March 10, 1817: *162*

The Writings of James Madison (Hunt ed. 1900–1910): *159, 160, 161, 162, 163, 172*

Writings of Washington (Fitzpatrick ed. 1938): *166*

The Writings of George Washington (Ford ed. 1891): *161*

INDEX

217

BAIL (*cont.*)
indigents, ill-effects of present system on, 157
release on own recognizance should replace present system, 157
unavailability of, makes presumption of innocence meaningless, 156–57

BALANCING PROCESS
Bill of Rights:
a product of, (Brant) 35; (Black) 60–61, 63
immune from, (Brant) 34–35; (Black) 45–63; (Warren) 109
historical background opposes, 35–37, 45–48
dangers of, (Brant) 34–35; (Black) 59–62; (Warren) 109
fictitious opinion illustrating (Black), 58–59
habeas corpus right, immune from (Black), 57
judicial discretion enhanced by (Black), 60
military necessity v. individual rights, 91, 95, 100–01
nation's interest in freedom is part of (Warren), 109, 111
objections to, (Brant), 34–36; (Black) 45–63; (Warren) 109, 111; (Douglas) 128–29
judicial review weakened by (Black), 60
legislative supremacy restored by, (Black) 60; (Douglas) 129
religious test prohibition immune from (Black), 57

supporters' view of, 44–45, 58–59, 131–32

BILL OF ATTAINDER. *See* Attainder, Bill of

BILL OF RIGHTS. *See also* Balancing Process; Bill of Rights, Application to Military; Bill of Rights, Application to States; Due Process of Law; Federal Government; First through Tenth Amendment; Government; Madison; Minority Rights
additional protections needed today (Douglas), 149, 155–56
adherence to, key to foreign policy success, 158
affirmative side of liberties omitted, 147
Alien and Sedition Acts opposed as contra, 37–38, 130–31
application influenced by value-judgments, 156
bill of attainder prohibition included in, (Brant) 31; (Black) 43–44
clear and present danger test qualifies, 44
Constitution's effectiveness depends upon, 4–5
court-made rules hinder enforcement of (Douglas), 133–41. *See also* Judicial Review
court-made rules safeguarding: narrow police power statute required, 140
void-for-vagueness doctrine, 140

BILL OF RIGHTS *(cont.)*
  debates, trustworthiness of Annals of Congress (Brant), 36, 43
  deepening sensitivity of Supreme Court toward, 9–11
  defined (Black), 43–44
  due process clause given content by (Douglas), 131
  effectiveness requires:
    consensus of people, 118–21
    constant effort of people, 11–12
    greater availability of judicial relief (Douglas), 133–41, 144–46, 150–51
    independent judiciary, 7–8, 36, 49–50, 62, 78, 91, 119–20
    support of church, 127; community leaders, 128, 155; lawyers, 127–28, 156; mass media, 124–27, 155
    universal understanding of, 153–56
  endangered by excessive fear for security, 111–12
  enforcement ignored by states, 85–86
  ex post facto law prohibition included in, (Brant) 31; (Black) 43–44
  federal standards go beyond demands of, 82
  framed as commands, not exhortations, 4
  habeas corpus right included in, (Brant) 31; (Black) 43–44
  historical background:
    amendment limiting states rejected, 34, 69–70, 78
    Convention's rejection of in-
      itial proposal explained, 31–32
    early distrust of democracy, 147
    indicates military necessity not grounds for disregarding, 102
    Madison drafts, 4, 16
    Madison's efforts to secure, 16, 32–36, 43
    Madison sponsors, 16, 33, 35, 43
    opposed to balancing, 36, 45–48
    revolutionary goals exceed traditional English rights, 3
    submitted by First Congress, 43
  inadequate to protect individual against government (Douglas), 144
  increased importance of, 121–25, 147–52
  intended as absolutes, (Brant) 34–36; (Black) 45–63; (Douglas) 129
  international importance of. *See also* Foreign Policy
    to assure freedom in new nations, 153–54, 157–58
  judicial interpretation weakens (Douglas), 120, 128–132
  judicial protection is recent undertaking, 8–11
  jury trial guarantee (Const) included in, (Brant) 31; (Black) 43
  limited instances of judicial enhancement of, 150–51
  Madison as source for understanding, 43
  Madison on, generally, 33, 35–36, 50, 62, 120

EVIDENCE *(cont.)*
Amendment; Fourth
Amendment; Search and
Seizure; Sixth Amendment
government claims of secrecy
thwart judiciary, 110
EXCLUSIONARY RULE, FEDERAL
need for in state criminal proceedings, 83, 131
not applicable to states, 83, 131
EXECUTIVE
control of industry:
inherent power and congressional mandate distinguished, 107–08
injunction of strikes, 108
paucity of precedent in court review of, 108
steel mill seizure, 107–08
wartime and peacetime distinguished, 107
exercise of discretion, need for greater review of (Douglas), 135
primary role in upholding Constitution (Warren), 112
war power, reaction to fear of military, 93
wide discretion as wartime necessity, 101
EX POST FACTO LAW
Bill of Rights includes prohibition of, (Brant) 31; (Black) 43–44
due to distrust of legislatures, 32
modern use of, 117

FEDERAL COURTS. *See* Judiciary
FEDERAL EMPLOYEES. *See also* Employment, Right to

active political participation denied to, 137
religious oath requirement, 57
security risk dismissals, 110, 150, 171
FEDERAL GOVERNMENT. *See also* Congress; Executive; Judiciary
Bill of Rights originally adopted to limit only, 44, 68
change from laissez faire to welfare state, 147
created by sovereign states, 67–68, 70
delegated powers, nature of, 68
FEDERALISM. *See* Division of Powers
FEDERALIST PAPERS
advocate of Constitution, 16, 28–29
authors of, 16, 28
Madison's contribution to, 16, 28–29
FIFTH AMENDMENT. *See also* Due Process of Law
all criminal procedure safeguards should apply to states (Brennan), 85
continued need for (Douglas), 155–56
double jeopardy prohibition should be applied to states, (Brant) 162; (Brennan) 85
due process provision:
Frankfurter on unimportance of, 118
meaning not agreed upon, 52–53
modern example of lack of, 118–19
same meaning under fourteenth amendment, 131

MAGNA CARTA (*cont.*)
 individual rights not secured
 by, 4, 56
 Parliament not limited by, 46–
 47, 49
 sovereignty of monarch implicit
 in, 5
MARSHALL, CHIEF JUSTICE JOHN
 necessary and proper clause defined, 161
 on Constitutional restraints
 upon states, 132
 on inapplicability of Bill of
 Rights to states, 71
 on reasons for judicial review,
 142–43
 on Virginia Declaration of
 Rights, 4
MASON, GEORGE
 motion for Bill of Rights, rejection by Convention explained, 31
MILITARY. *See also* Bill of Rights,
 Application to Military;
 Civilian Supremacy over
 Military; Courts Martial;
 Defense effort, Effect on
 Civilian Life.
 authority over civilians:
 broad judicial review of, 99–
 106
 denied where civil courts
 open, 100, 106
 requires express congressional
 directives, 106, 170
 selective service violations
 not subject to, 170
 authority over own personnel:
 desertion not grounds for de-
 nationalization, 10, 99
 fundamental rights guaranteed, 97–99
 limited judicial review of,
 95–99

pre-induction activities not
 grounds for nonhonorable
 discharge, 105
 recall for purpose of court
 martial prohibited, 104–05
claims of necessity must be
 tested (Warren), 102–04,
 106
conscientious objector, rights
 of, 170
constitutional provisions
 prompted by fear of, 93
courts ill-equipped to evaluate
 actions of, 96
dangers of coalition with industry, 112–13, 171
freedom endangered by excessive judicial deference to,
 102, 106, 136
ideological instruction of
 troops, 11
ideological supervision of civilian personnel unreview-
 able, 150
increased size raises new legal
 questions, 96–97, 99, 104,
 105
judicial review of, limited, 91,
 112
procurement activities, review
 of, 111
threat to democratic society,
 90–93
veterans' benefits, expansion of,
 110–11, 171
wartime and peacetime discretion contrasted, 100–05
withholding of pay requires
 legislative authority, 170
MILITARY APPEALS, COURT OF
 safeguards servicemen's rights,
 97–98
MINORITY RIGHTS
 Bill of Rights protects, 50, 62